LIFE SINCE 1900

Life
Since 1900

CHARLES FURTH

London
GEORGE ALLEN & UNWIN LTD
RUSKIN HOUSE MUSEUM STREET

for A H F

By the same author

YOU AND THE STATE

YOUR WORK AND WAGES
with *Sally Graves*

———

REVISED EDITION

First published in July 1956
Second impression December 1956
Third impression (Second Edition) 1960
Fourth Impression (Third Edition) 1966

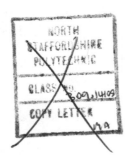

PRINTED IN GREAT BRITAIN
BY PHOTOLITHOGRAPHY
UNWIN BROTHERS LIMITED
WOKING AND LONDON

PREFACE

N O previous period of human history has known change as fundamental and as rapid as in the first sixty odd years of this century. Until now change has generally taken place at about the same rate as a man changes, so that he has noticed nothing startling in his lifetime. But in the last sixty years the rate of change has been violently accelerated. As a young man Sir Winston Churchill took part in a cavalry charge in which his troopers were armed with sabre and lance; he survived to grapple with the problem of the hydrogen bomb.

Many of us, looking back, see the period before 1914 in the golden haze of a lost leisure, of a gracious and unhurried way of living. It seems always to have been gentle summer. But of course it was not. There were also winters of sulphurous fog in which the poor were known to collapse on the streets. The First World War separates us from this period by a great gulf. It was followed by a time of irritable and difficult readjustment after the strain and slaughter of the war, culminating in the General Strike of 1926. This is the period of the febrile bright young things who introduced night-clubs, jazz and West End treasure-hunts. The nineteen-thirties then saw the grim insecurity of the world trade depression. And these twenty years between the two world wars were probably the formative period of their lives for many of those who are still only middle-aged, who have brought up families and whose opinions count in the community. Between us and that inter-war period is stretched the great gulf of the Second World War.

What I have attempted is to paint portraits of Britain before the First World War and of Britain between the wars, and to trace what changed the first into the second and the latter into the different society we inhabit to-day. The book makes no claim to original research. Nor does it attempt to analyse in any detail such difficult abstractions as the changing intellectual climate or the literature of the time. Apart from gleanings from periodicals over a period of years, it is based on standard works and on contemporary books which are still readily accessible. My reason for attempting the task with such modest equipment was that, when it was first written, I could not find, amongst the political, social and economic histories, the memoirs and analytical studies, that just this had been done before in this elementary form. Yet it is important, for without an understanding of the past, the present seems even more bewildering than it is.

In this new edition I have brought the book up-to-date, revising figures and comments and trying to live up to the open-ended promise of its title. Much of the chapters on 'The World To-day' and on 'The Social Revolution' is rewritten. But I have not attempted any commentary on man's space flights. This is partly because they are in the daily news, partly because—albeit the peak of man's technical achievement—what they now contribute (other than to national prestige) can only be assessed by the scientist and their ultimate importance is still veiled by Time. The 1956 edition of this book is, however, a minor indication of the breathless speed of advance. To describe the outlook of scientists in the nineteen-twenties it rashly commented that to them the use of atomic power seemed as remote as to us 'travelling by rocket into space'.

CONTENTS

ILLUSTRATIONS

9

A Lost World

1900–1914

THE upper classes gave to the Edwardian years a brilliance and glitter which to-day we see only on the films. This was a life of frank privilege. Social status derived from the old landed aristocracy, which had freely intermarried and strengthened itself with the wealthy manufacturers of the nineteenth century, and now the purse-strings were loosened, the insistence on the ploughing back of profits was no longer so great and the strict Victorian code was relaxed under King Edward. During the London season there were magnificent social gatherings almost nightly in Mayfair, whose summer scent, 'compounded of warm earth in the square gardens and horse-dung and lime leaves', was heavy also with the fragrance of flowers sent up to grace the ballrooms from the hothouses of the country estates. As yet there were no petrol fumes, the clip-clop of horses' hooves was still the traffic's usual sound as the broughams and landaus set down their guests by the red carpet leading from the pavement's edge, past the footmen and up the steps to the foot of the stately stairway, at the head of which the guest's name would be announced in ringing tones to his welcoming hosts. Not until the dawn was breaking over London, and the street-cleaners were out with their hoses, would the dancers break up and seek their beds.

But although one came to London for the season, the basis of aristocratic life was still, as it had always been in England, the countryside. Of the county houses Mr. Gore writes in his *Edwardian Scrapbook*:[1]

[1] London, Evans Bros., 1951.

'Summer or winter, indoors and out, their charms were inescapable. To wake early and from bedroom window to drink in the scents and sounds and loveliness of a famous garden; to ride before breakfast during a cricket week, cantering across some lovely park, through rides in the green bracken, startling the deer and the rabbits and brushing the dew from the turf. Those velvet lawns, sloping to the river or the lake, the music of waterfowl and song-birds, the long, long hours of pleasant games and company, the ordered luxury and plenty of punctual meals and silent service. . . .

'Pleasant in those days–never before or since so pleasant–it was to be a son of such a house. For outwardly always, and in great part sincerely, loyally and wholeheartedly, all who ministered to the family were in league to spoil the golden youths when they returned home from Oxford or Eton. The butler, the head keeper, the coachman and the stud-groom, old and tried friends all, had stored up pleasant surprises; the old nanny, the cook and the maids had long been preparing for the happy return. His young lordship's hunter was in trim, Master Charles's pony was bursting with oats, the fishing keeper had his jealous eye on "the two-pound trout below the lasher"; or the "outsides" were ripe to be shot and Master Charles's place would be at the gap in that spinney where he got his first woodcock last year; and his new 16-bore was ready for him. There were holiday delights ahead for every day of the winter and summer holidays, and in those delights, on field and river and cricket ground, servers and served shared equally in pride and pleasure.'

'Stable parade' followed morning service in the village church: 'The straw edges of the litter were still beautifully plaited; the selected and well-washed carrots were still laid out on the ledge, and the fat carriage horses, bursting with oats, Lady Mary's cob and his lordship's hunters and Master Charles's pony still whinnied and stamped and looked greedily around.'

For the upper middle classes too it was a thoroughly comfortable time in which life ran smoothly and without physical effort. There was no scarcity of trained and skilful servants, nor did their services cost an undue proportion of one's income; there were no shortages of goods which even money could not buy, nor were there obstacles which even money could not put aside. It seems to us barely credible that in those days one could travel abroad without even a passport: it was simply a question of booking one's rooms, buying a ticket and taking a cab to Victoria Station. And it went even subtly further: at holiday resorts, both home and abroad, one found only a sprinkling of one's own sort–the others did not take a holiday.

One of the things we notice most in the pre-war world, alongside its division into clearly defined social classes, is the cohesion within each class, the active social intercourse between families, the frequency with which they went into each other's homes. Mr. Gore quotes the contemporary diary of a senior civil servant entertaining his circle of friends at small dinner-parties of ten or twelve regularly every week from early February until the end of July and being entertained by them on an average twice a week. This active, gracious and intricately regulated social life, these formal dinners with good amateur music, the large luncheon-parties at week-ends, the tennis- and garden-parties in summer, complete with little marquees or tents, all this depended upon a plethora of household servants. It was they who made possible the ceremony of afternoon tea, with the polished silver teapot and the little bell one rang for more hot water, the endless starched and frilled underclothes, the warm, cosy nursery teas with nanny, the colourful ritual of the dancing class, above all the sense of security and order, of unhurried, gracious parents which live so strongly in the memories of those brought up in comfortable Edwardian households.

There is a characteristically charming glimpse of the well-to-do middle-class lady and her maid in Mrs. Gwen Raverat's memoir: 'Ladies were ladies in those days; they did not do things themselves, they told other people what to do and how to do it. . . . Aunt Etty was most emphatically such a person. She told me, when she was eighty-six, that she had never made a pot of tea in her life; and that she had never in all her days been out in the dark alone, not even in a cab; and I don't believe she had ever travelled by train without a maid. She certainly always took her maid with her when she went in a fly to the dentist's. . . . I am sure that she had never sewn on a button, and I should guess

that she had hardly ever even posted a letter herself. . . . Once
she wrote when her maid, the patient and faithful Janet, was away
for a day or two: "I am very busy answering my own bell." And
I can well believe it, for Janet's work was no sinecure. But, of
course, while Janet was away, the housemaid was doing all the
real work; and Aunt Etty was only perhaps finding the postage
stamps for herself, or putting on her own shawl–the sort of
things she rang for Janet to do, every five minutes all day long.'[1]

This was the period too of the nanny, the grown-up who could
devote herself almost entirely to the child, could move at the
child's pace, placid, generally without much in the way of education and certainly untroubled by psychological theories. Undis-
turbed by other responsibilities, she pushed the pram along the
pavement and into the park, or up the hill and out to the fields,
telling an endless story to the elder child trotting beside her, or
gossiping with some other nanny. These servants, moreover, had
their professional skill and pride. Maybe their devotion to the
family they served owed more than they knew to the scarcity in
the early years of the century of other employment for women,
particularly in the south, but devoted they most often were.
And their cost? At the beginning of the century a butler earned
rather more than £58 yearly, a domestic servant in London about
£18 (rather less elsewhere), for a girl under sixteen a yearly
wage of £8 was normal, in addition to keep and uniform. It is
true that already in 1909 we read a complaint about 'domestic
servants, now so difficult to get, and so exacting when found'. Yet
even in 1931 there were nearly four times as many as were left
in 1951.

The Edwardian period too was the heyday of life in middle-
class suburbia. To us Acacia Avenue and Laburnum Grove,
'Holmlea', 'Buena Vista', 'Sunnyhurst' and 'The Laurels' are only
part of that drab and unfamiliar wilderness of brick boxes (unfamiliar except for our own little corner) which separates the
city centre from the remote green fields. But in those days they
were bright and new, their gardens neat and trim, not yet encircled by inter-war suburbs and municipal housing-estates.
Family life was strong, with the small, generally semi-detached

[1] Gwen Raverat, *Period Piece* (Faber, 1952).

house as its centre, its front garden a sort of antechamber to the pavement beyond, for it was on the pavement that the children of suburbia spent their best hours with scooter or tricycle, roller-skates or hoop. Little girls in those days were 'white and bunchy',[1] with pigtails and long black legs like spiders, while little boys were nearly always navy blue: either clad in a blue jersey or else in a blue sailor suit.

In the early days of the century it was a disgrace to play games on a Sunday, but as Victorian strictness faded into a more easy-going way of life the click of the croquet ball was heard on the suburban back lawn both on Sunday and on Saturday afternoon. There was also an indoor variety of the game to be played in bad weather on a green baize cloth spread on the dining-room table. Later badminton became more popular out of doors, although the English weather is unkind to the feathered shuttlecock, which was liable to be blown over the garden wall: indeed one variant of the game might be played with the neighbour on the other side. A conscious sense of community then united the neat little houses of these suburban streets. Amateur dramatics, music, tennis, all flourished in local clubs, often connected with the church. They were not then reduced to their present anaemia by mechanised amusement and the attraction of the centre, towards which modern transport so easily draws blood from the suburbs.

The lower middle-class family, however, was more self-contained, less socially at ease with its neighbours, for it was anxiously concerned to preserve its distinction from the working class. 'I think grimly', writes Mr. Richard Church, 'of the small margin of safety which my parents struggled to maintain between their respectable little home and the hungry ocean of violence whose thunder never left our ears; the violence of the street, the crass mob, the ever-rising waters of the indifferent masses,' and he instances one of the brutal scenes of drunken fighting which a child might then see in the streets.[2]

Mr. Church lived in a working-class district, but we find the same anxiety among the humbler members of the great middle

---

[1] The phrase is Mr. James Kenward's in his delightful picture of childhood in the great days of middle-class suburbia, *The Suburban Child* (Cambridge, 1955).
[2] *Over the Bridge* (Heinemann, 1955).

classes living in the new suburbs. The social reforms of the early years of the century, following on those instigated by the late Victorian conscience, already carried the first threat to the superior status of the clerk, the teacher, the white-collared worker in general, as against that of the artisan. Masterman writes in 1909: 'And the taxes thus extorted–this, perhaps, is the heart of the complaint–are all going to make his own life harder, to make life more difficult for his children. The man of forty has already sounding in his ears the clamour of the coming generations. And these coming generations, who are going to push him roughly out of his occupation, and bring his little castle in ruins to the ground, are being provided with an equipment for the struggle out of the funds which he himself is compelled to supply.'[1] (Secondary-school places per 1,000 of the population approximately doubled between 1895 and 1910–and then almost trebled between 1910 and 1938. And one of the regulations issued by the Liberal President of the Board of Education in 1907 which caused concern in middle-class circles was that obliging secondary schools which accepted a grant-in-aid at the higher available rate to give 25 per cent of their places free to scholarship winners from the public elementary schools.)

Turn now from 'The Laurels' and 'Sunnyhurst' to the typical working-class dwelling of the period. 'One type of dwelling, indeed, is to be found more or less prevalent through all the urban agglomeration. That is the small four- or five-roomed cottage, containing on the ground floor a front parlour, a kitchen, and a scullery built as an addition to the main part of the house; and on the upper floor the bedrooms, the third bedroom in the five-roomed house being built over the scullery . . .' '. . . that enormous acreage of chimney-pots and tiny tumbled cottages which is revealed in a kind of smoky grandeur from the railway embankments of South and East London–the desperate efforts made by a race reared in village communities to maintain in the urban aggregation some semblance of a home.'[2]

[1] C. F. G. Masterman, *The Condition of England* (Methuen). We now take it for granted that secondary education of some sort is available to everyone.

[2] Masterman, *op. cit.* The rearguard of these are still in use, despite inter-war slum clearance and war-time bombing, and are still a familiar sight, interspersed with 'prefabs' and modern council flats, to those who daily flood into the centre from London's now remote outer suburbs.

Or here is an extract from the report of one of Mr. Rowntree's team who made house-to-house enquiries in York in 1899. The home described is that of a man with two children, in the lowest-paid group (22s. a week) but in regular employment.

'The house is clean and comfortable. It consists of two rooms. The front door opens into a tiny hall, about four feet square, and the stairs to the bedroom rise out of this. In the living-room is a sideboard with a table, an easy-chair, and one or two other chairs; a wringing machine and a perambulator stand in one corner; by the fireside is the baby's wooden cradle. The cooking is done in this room and the bread baked here. . . . The pantry is an unventilated cupboard under the stairs. From the living-room a small passage leads to the back yard, which contains the sanitary conveniences and water-tap. These are shared with one other house. The "copper" for washing clothes is in this yard, and stands in the open air. In wet or rough weather this must add considerably to the usual discomforts of washing days.'[1]

Lady Bell's contemporary picture[2] of working-class life in Middlesbrough is painted from the employer's angle with intimate knowledge, but without sentiment or patronising. It shows a life devoted to unremitting work throughout its adult years. There are no holidays and little amusement. (Except for foremen, holidays with pay were almost unknown.) Average working hours in 1909 were fifty-five per week, with longer hours in many trades not regulated by Factory Acts. Year in, year out, Sunday is the only day off: the man often spends most of it in bed, smoking and reading lurid newspapers; the woman can never completely escape from housework and children. They never get out of the neighbourhood and their homes are dark—because built so close together, at the expense of all privacy—inconvenient and overcrowded, put up as quickly as possible to keep pace with the rapid expansion of the works. (In 1831 the population of Middlesbrough was 154; in 1901, 91,302.) Frequently there is an unmarried lodger in addition to the family.

---

[1] Rowntree, *Poverty* (Longmans, Green & Co., 1900).
[2] Lady Bell, *At the Works, A Study of a Manufacturing Town* (Arnold, 1907).

B

'Any lapse from self-denial, from temperance, from economy, from civility even . . . at once and swiftly brings about a deplorable result.' She writes of 'the desperate, tense strain of incessant economy'. There is never a margin for a spree and seldom even for an error in buying. Work generally continues as long as it is physically possible. 'Over and over again one finds such instances: a man is doing the work of a labourer, perhaps, in his old age, at 18s. a week, who has been in receipt of twice or even three times that amount when he was younger.' With, before 1908, not even a modest statutory pension, 'old age . . . must indeed look dark when it represents either destitution or dependence'.

The vitality of the women was often sapped by frequent pregnancies. 'One woman had had seventeen children and twelve had died; another fourteen, of whom eight had died. One woman had had ten still-born children, in addition to which four more were born alive.' At any rate during that long stretch of years in which there were always small children in the home the mother's life was generally a continuous struggle against exhaustion—a struggle of which, in a less acute degree, the middle-class woman with young children has now become uncomfortably aware. Outside his work, even the workman in a responsible position was oddly ill-at-ease in his own civilisation, unfamiliar with the idea of sending a letter and quite unable to contemplate using the telephone (invented already in 1875). The womenfolk were even more restricted in experience and outlook.

Desperately narrow was the margin which separated from actual want and hunger even the thoroughly sober workman who was in regular employment. It needed only a prolonged illness and that margin was crossed. Lady Bell takes the case of 'a very competent workman, Jack D. The household consisted of the husband and wife and two daughters in their teens. This man, who had a delicate chest, caught a chill at the funeral of one of his mates. His wife begged him next morning not to go to his work. But he insisted on going all the same, as he did not want to lose a day's pay. He was not working on the eight-hour shift; his hours every day were from 6 a.m. to 6 p.m. . . . He was after this off work for several weeks, which meant that during all that

time he earned nothing, and that what they had to live upon was
15s. a week from two sick clubs to which he had subscribed, and
such meagre savings as they had been able to effect out of 36s. a
week. Besides this a "gathering", that is, a collection, had been
made at the works for him by his fellows among themselves,
amounting to some £5, contributed with the unfailing generosity
always shown by the men under such circumstances. . . . Afterwards, when the long weeks of illness were over, during the
man's weary, dragging convalescence, when the resources of the
savings and of the "gathering" had come to an end and the 15s.
from the sick clubs was all that remained, the house still looked
as clean and spotless, the wife was as uncomplaining, and the
whole household as peaceful as before. And the visitor who went
to that house came away with the indelible impression of the
aspect of the worn and pale wife, almost at the end of her strength
after the weeks of nursing and privation, and now face to face
with the mortal anxiety for the future, still presenting a front
of courage and cheerfulness'.

We have already moved a long way from the great houses in
Mayfair and the 3,937 pheasants shot by King Edward and six
other guns in one day. But we are still only with the decent workman in regular employment. We have not yet plumbed the abyss,
and descent into the abyss was easy in those days when social
security was barely the beginnings of an idea. Unemployment,
accident, illness, the death of the wage-earner, old age: these
are still the causes of the remaining poverty found by Mr.
Rowntree in 1950; before the First World War they could mean
disaster.

In 1903 Jack London sewed a golden guinea into his vest, as a
sort of financial life-belt; formally advised the American Consul
in London of his hazardous intentions; fitted himself out from a
pawnbroker's shop in the then distinctive clothing of the working
man, and submerged himself, with his notebook, in the East
End of London. He describes conditions in the 'sweated trades'—
trades in which desperate competition for work caused men and
women labouring in their own homes and often with their own
equipment to produce clothes, shoes, etc., for outside employers
at starvation prices—before the Trade Boards Act of 1909. 'Passing

Leman Street, we cut off to the left into Spitalfields, and dived into Frying-pan Alley. . . . Up we went, three flights, each landing two feet by three in area, and heaped with filth and refuse. . . .

'In six of the rooms, twenty-odd people, of both sexes and all ages, cooked, ate, slept and worked. In size the rooms averaged eight feet by eight, or possibly nine. The seventh room we entered. It was the den in which five men "sweated". It was seven feet wide by eight long, and the table at which the work was performed took up the major portion of the space. On this table were five lasts, and there was barely room for the men to stand to their work, for the rest of the space was heaped with cardboard, leather, bundles of shoe uppers, and a miscellaneous assortment of materials used in attaching the uppers of shoes to their soles. . . .

'My sweated friend, when work was to be had, toiled with four other men in his eight-by-seven room. In the winter a lamp burned nearly all the day and added its fumes to the overloaded air, which was breathed, and breathed, and breathed again.

'In good times, when there was a rush of work, this man told me that he could earn as high as "thirty bob a week". . . . "But it's only the best of us can do it," he qualified. "An' then we work twelve, thirteen and fourteen hours a day, just as fast as we can. An' you should see us sweat! Just running from us! If you could see us, it'd dazzle your eyes—tacks flyin' out of mouth like from a machine. Look at my mouth." I looked. The teeth were worn down by the constant friction of the metallic brads, while they were coal-black and rotten. "I clean my teeth," he added, "else they'd be worse". . . .'[1]

At that time, in the slums, it was not uncommon to see an advertisement for part of a room to let, and in some cases beds were let on a three-relay system—that is, three tenants to a bed, each occupying it eight hours, so that it never grew cold. Jack London gives a typical example of a room let on the more respectable two-relay system. During the day it was occupied by a woman who worked all night in a hotel. When she went out to work at seven in the evening a bricklayer's labourer came in.

[1] Jack London, *People of the Abyss* (Isbister, 1903).

At seven in the morning, when he went to work, she returned from hers.

Such were the conditions when poverty was left to find its own level, except for charity and the workhouse. The hospitality granted by the workhouse, under the old Poor Law, was deliberately intended to be hospitality of a deterrent kind. The lot of those dependent on parish relief was meant to be inferior to that of those in employment, for it was still the prevailing philosophy that poverty was the result of vice, improvidence or laziness. (And when in 1906 a Departmental Earnings Enquiry gave average weekly wages in the cotton trade as 29s. 6d., jute 21s. 7d., public utilities 28s. 1d., agriculture–allowing for the labourer's receipts in kind–about 20s., while Rowntree reckoned the minimum required for bare subsistence by a family of five at 21s. 8d., the upper limit of the workhouse provision was not very high.) Moreover, even to get into a workhouse involved starting to queue about noon, which left little time for breaking out from the vicious circle by finding work. It was, however, then–and it still is–illegal to sleep out at night in the streets without visible means of support; you can only do so if you can show that you have the price of a bed on you. Consequently those who slept out underneath railway arches, in doorways and odd corners, were liable to be constantly 'moved on' by the police, for to *walk* the streets all night is not illegal. But if you walk all night you must sleep in the day. 'We went up the narrow gravelled walk. On the benches on either side arrayed a mass of miserable and distorted humanity. . . . A chill, raw wind was blowing, and these creatures, huddled there in their rags, sleeping for the most part, or trying to sleep. Here were a dozen women, ranging in age from twenty years to seventy. Next a babe, possibly of nine months, lying asleep, flat on the hard bench, with neither pillow nor covering, nor with anyone looking after it. Next half a dozen men, sleeping bolt upright or leaning against one another in their sleep. In one place a family group, a child asleep in its sleeping mother's arms, and the husband . . . clumsily mending a dilapidated shoe.'[1]

Small wonder that in these conditions Rowntree in York found

---

[1] Jack London, *op. cit.*

'mortality amongst the very poor . . . more than twice as high as amongst the best-paid section of the working class', or that Jack London could assert that in London's East End 55 per cent of children died before the age of five, as against at that time 18 per cent in the West End. In the gardens of London's aristocratic squares 'the golden babes and lassies, properly attended, played inside in summer, and the mews and slum children thrust their noses through the bars'.[1]

[1] John Gore, *op. cit.*

2

The Edwardian Heritage

W HAT lay behind the picture painted in the last chapter by so freely borrowing contemporary paint brushes? There was justification for spending so long in the towns, for by the turn of the century already 77 per cent of the population of England and Wales was urban. Yet up to 1880 Britain led the world in agriculture as clearly as in industry, and agriculture employed incomparably more people than any other single occupation. It was in the late 'seventies that American prairie-grown wheat first entered Europe in large quantities. Three changes took place about the same time, and together they proved decisive. The one which took place on the prairie itself was the development of agricultural machinery and particularly of the self-binder attached to the reaping machine. This made it possible for one man to work the machine alone, instead of with an assistant. Land was unlimited; the virgin soil needed no manures, no intensive cultivation. Manpower alone was the limiting factor, and the result of freeing the second man from the reaper was virtually to double the output.

Between 1860 and 1880 the railways in the United States more than trebled their mileage. Most of this prodigious expansion was across the prairies, and the railway companies were willing to carry grain at less than cost in order to encourage farmers to settle in the vast empty spaces they had so boldly spanned. The result of this second change was that grain could be cheaply carried eastwards. The fitting out of steamships with the compound engine and condenser completed the picture: in 1873 the cost of sending a ton of grain from Chicago to Liverpool was £3 7s.; by 1884 it had fallen to £1 4s. Moreover, the blow struck the British farmer at the worst time. The years 1875–9 saw a series of wet summers; world trade depression had reduced prices for meat and dairy produce; in 1877, 1879 and 1883 their cattle and sheep suffered from severe epidemics.

By 1879 every European country west of Russia had either to put a tariff on imported wheat or else see its own wheatfields go out of cultivation. Every wheat-growing country chose the tariff except the two most industrialised, Britain and Belgium. As Ensor writes, in 1879 'British agriculture . . . was thrown over-board in a storm like an unwanted cargo'.[1] In 1877 English wheat had fetched an average of 56s. 9d. per quarter; by 1886 only 31s. As a result, by 1900 English farmers ploughed little more than half the acreage of 1872. Rider Haggard gave it as his opinion in 1902 that only two kinds of farming could pay in Britain: that of the large man with capital, basing his farming on grass (and imported cattle cake), producing milk and prime meat; or that of the small man employing only his own family. The only way to make a living was, in his view, to sell liquid milk, market-garden produce, pigs and poultry fed on imported grain.

Hitherto, despite its industrialisation, the tone of the country, as of every other country, had been set by agriculture. The harvest had coloured the year and was its main event. The British people were not then divorced from the soil. Now, farming ceased to be of any real importance in the life of the nation. The population of London, that great wen, doubled between 1851 and 1908; eighty-four large urban areas increased their population nearly threefold, while that of fourteen rural counties (excluding their large towns) decreased by 5 per cent.

Masterman wrote in 1909: 'Whole ancient skilled occupations –hedging and ditching, the traditional treatment of beasts and growing things–are becoming lost arts in rural England. Behind the appearance of a feverish prosperity and adventure–motors along the main roads, golf-courses, gamekeepers, gardeners, armies of industrious servants, excursionists, hospitable enter-tainment of country house-parties–we can discern the passing of a race of men.'[2] Or again he writes of a great silence that broods over a doomed and passing race, that of the rural labourer, whose

---

[1] R. C. K. Ensor, England, 1870–1914 (Oxford, 1936).
[2] C. F. G. Masterman, The Condition of England (1909).

children are 'vanishing from the life of open sky into the mazes of the lamplit city', where Rowntree met them in York and Jack London in the slums of Shoreditch.

Since that time Britain has imported most of her food. One main part of the pattern of our lives as we live them in mid-twentieth century was already determined by Edwardian times. From then on our food depended on our exports of coal and manufactures, on shipping, insurance, banking and similar 'services'.

In Edwardian times our exports were still vast and were still increasing (total British exports were worth £291 million in 1900 and £525 million in 1913), but American and German production was increasing more rapidly than ours. 'Our position in the race of civilised nations is no longer what it has been,' said the Chancellor of the Exchequer as early as 1888. 'We have had a great start in industry and commerce, and by virtue of that start we have attained to a station of unprecedented and long un-challenged supremacy. That supremacy is no longer unchallenged. Others are pressing on our heels.'

The industrial depression of the eighteen-eighties followed on that of the eighteen-seventies and agriculture remained de-pressed all the time. The word 'unemployed' first appeared in the Oxford English Dictionary in 1882. In November 1905 Queen Alexandra issued a public appeal: 'I appeal to all charitably disposed people in the Empire, both men and women, to assist me in alleviating the suffering of the poor starving unemployed during the winter. For this purpose I head the list with £2,000.' The sun which had blazed so warmly on British industry in its brilliant noon continued to shine, but the sky was never cloudless again. The United States began to outstrip us in the use of machinery; British factories failed to keep pace in substituting the flexible electric motor for the massive steam engine with its shafts and belting. Signs of relative decline emerge readily enough from the figures. In the eighteen-seventies Britain produced about half the world's pig-iron; on the eve of the First World War only about one-eighth. In steel production she was outdistanced before 1914 by the U.S.A. and Germany; after the Second War by the U.S.S.R.

Only in shipping and shipbuilding did we retain our remarkable preponderance. And there was one compensation for what we had lost, for Britain became more than ever the world's warehouseman, banker and financial agent. One result of this was the increase in the number of clerks. They joined the expanding army of the middle class. Between 1901 and 1911 the number of clerks increased by nearly a third, although population only rose by 10 per cent; in the next twenty years the number of those earning their living by paper work almost doubled (although the total employed population only increased by 15 per cent). Not all of those included in this last figure were clerks. It covers the professions and the growing body of technicians—all those not employed in manual labour. Nevertheless it measures the extent to which in Britain 'the office' was replacing 'the works'. And of those clerks an increasing proportion were women: in 1891 only 8 per cent were grudgingly admitted (with all proper safeguards), in 1901 18 per cent, by 1911 32 per cent of 'clerks' were women. The telephone and the typewriter brought women into the offices, hitherto the preserve of men—bewhiskered, top-hatted, frock-coated.

The Victorians had large families. Seven or eight children were common, but after 1877 birth-control began to be effective, and it was most noticeable amongst the most highly educated. The Edwardian professional and business man did not intend to have more than two or three children, although the working-class mother—for lack of knowledge and opportunity to apply what knowledge she had—continued to bear more. (The 'one-child family' still lay ahead in the 'thirties.) This fall in the size of upper- and middle-class families had far-reaching effects. There was no longer the same need for the large Victorian house, with its big nursery upstairs, its massive dining-room table (very suitable for ping-pong), its many servants. It also gave more free time to mothers. But for the father also the upbringing and support of his family became a less exacting and absorbing task. There was, in the upper classes, more time for amusement; the Victorian drive began to slacken. Although the standard working week remained one of *six* nine-hour days right up to 1914, office hours shortened after about 1900 and some of our grandparents began to enjoy the free Saturday afternoon, the 'English week-end'. They followed the example of Parliament, which discontinued its Saturday-afternoon session in 1903. Between 1889 and 1897 over 500 establishments adopted the forty-eight-hour week of six *eight*-hour days, but it did not become general until after 1918. The birth-rate continued to fall between 1900 and 1914, the effect of its fall being balanced by a reduction in the rate of deaths, particularly among children. (This infant death-rate averaged 15 per cent of the live births between 1841 and 1870, but had fallen by one-third to 10 per cent in 1910. The rate in 1954 was 2.64 per cent.)

As one would expect from its middle-class population, the birth-rate in suburbia was below the average for towns. And suburbia was growing rapidly, for there was a building boom between 1900 and 1910 and much of it was on the outskirts of towns—Laburnum Grove and Acacia Avenue were then being built. This new building drained off the comparatively well-to-do, leaving the old buildings, in the town centres, to be filled by those with less to spend. The outward movement was carried by the electric tram, which, together with electric light, was a late Victorian legacy. By the last years of the nineteenth century almost every provincial town of sufficient size possessed its trams —clean, swift and cheap. Generally they were owned by the town, for one of the last great achievements of Victoria's reign was to set up the structure of democratic local government as we still know it to-day (but now the areas of local administration are in need of change). London lagged behind the general movement and until 1905 the City and West End still depended upon horse-drawn omnibuses, so that to come to the capital from Manchester or Liverpool was to go back to the Victorian world, although London had its first Tube as early as 1890.[1] At the beginning of our period the motor-car was still generally a toy for the wealthy, and in fact it aggravated class feeling when these juggernauts tore at 10 m.p.h. down the narrow country roads, unpaved and unsuited to them, covering the hedges and all passers-by in a coat of white dust. But in 1905 the first motor-omnibuses appeared

---

[1] London 'was still a city of gaslight, of steam trains, of horse-buses, of four-wheelers and hansoms'.–D. W. Brogan in *History Today*.

in London and speedily drove out the horse-buses. Soon the horse was to become a rarity in cities, and with the horse went the crossing-sweeper.

The building boom relieved overcrowding, but there was still great poverty in the towns. The surveys of Booth and Rowntree indicated that nearly one-third of the population was unable to afford enough to eat. In his famous book *Riches and Poverty* L. Chiozza Money pointed out that almost *half* the national income went to only one-*ninth* of the population. His book made a sensation, averaging two printings a year between 1905 and 1910. The industrial revolution of the eighteenth and nineteenth centuries had conferred immense benefits upon the nation—had alone made it possible to support the vastly increased population—but this violent reshaping of society was a painful process for the then defenceless working classes. In earlier times the State had unquestioningly regulated labour conditions—as, for instance, in the Elizabethan Statute of Artificers. But the eight-hour day for miners, enacted in 1908, marked the end of a period of nearly one hundred years during which the State had not concerned itself with the working conditions of adult men. Mr. Churchill's Trade Boards Act of 1909 successfully abolished the sweat shops, such as the one described by Jack London, but it only covered four trades and only attacked that specific abuse. The trade unions, freed from the Combination Acts in 1824,[1] were at first interested only in the skilled artificer and mechanic. It was not until the great strikes of 1911 and 1912 that the big general trade unions began to organise the mass of unskilled men and to agitate effectively for better conditions. To us the power of the trade unions is so much a matter of course that we can hardly feel our way back to a period when employers could refuse to recognise them.[2]

The gradual stirring of the social conscience, the awareness of what Britain's dominance cost, can also be traced to the late

[1] Until that date all working-class organisations for the improvement of wages and conditions were regarded by the courts as criminal conspiracies.

[2] 'Further, they (the employers) will not under any circumstances consent to any recognition of the Union or Transport Workers Federation ticket, or to any discussion for such recognition'—from a letter sent to the Government in 1912 by the Port of London employers. The boot is now firmly on the other foot. The strong line then taken by the ship-owners is discussed in Chapter 10.

Victorian years. There was indeed an increasing uncertainty, not only in the sphere of industry and trade but also in morals. The Victorian giants derived much of their strength from a conviction that they knew what was right and what was wrong. But in the new century this certainty gave way to a comparative outlook, the beginnings of that 'relativism' which is typical of our time. We no longer take our stand so easily on absolute moral principle but tend to consider the circumstances in which an act was committed, the past experience and mental condition of the man concerned. The new outlook certainly led to a more constructive and enlightened approach to the problem of crime, beginning with the Prison Act of 1898, leading, in 1907, to the release of prisoners on probation and, in 1908, to the experiment of the Borstal system. In that year the Children Act ended the imprisonment of children under 14 (and strictly limited it under 16). An Act of 1914 greatly reduced the prison population by allowing reasonable time for the payment of fines.

The Church of England had lost its domination over men's minds in the thirty years before Victoria died, although the Nonconformist churches retained their hold with much greater success. Sincere belief became rare in the middle and upper classes, family prayers in the morning—with all the servants present—were dying out, or when continued were often an empty ritual, all too liable to be interrupted by the telephone. Psychology, the study and comparison of other religions, the study of primitive man and of the origins of his beliefs all contributed to a change of outlook. So also did the increased knowledge of our own bodies resulting from the advance of science and the surgeons' ability, after Lister's time, to penetrate much farther into the living organism. It was realised that hormones and the secretions of ductless glands affect behaviour. In short, conduct was seen to be conditioned by the chemistry of the body as well as by its owner's morals.

A much more questionable Victorian legacy was that of the sensationalist popular Press. The prototype was appropriately named *Tit-Bits*, started in 1880. It catered for the millions to whom the Education Act of 1870 and the subsequently created system of compulsory public education was teaching reading, without going on to teach them its uses. The *Daily Mail*, launched in 1896, soon had a circulation more than twice that of any other English daily. Of its founder, later Lord Northcliffe, an intimate biographer wrote: 'Boyish the limited range of his intellect, which seldom concerns itself with anything but the immediate, the obvious, the popular. Boyish his irresponsibility, his disinclination to take himself or his publications seriously; his conviction that whatever benefits them is justifiable, and that it is not his business to consider the effect of their contents on the public mind.'[1] These new popular newspapers were out for the maximum profitable circulation. It was, and is, their criterion of success. They were edited with great skill so as to appeal to the widest possible readership, which meant seeking the lowest common denominator amongst readers, and this was generally discovered to be sensationalism, sex and jingoism. The newspapers of the old days—edited with a greater sense of responsibility—had printed telegrams and reports pretty well as their correspondents sent them in. The new popular papers spiced and peppered their stories, cut them into short paragraphs and gave them lively headings. To quote Mr. Ensor again, 'the old method served up its news raw, while the new one served it cooked'.

The battle against illiteracy had been won before the end of the nineteenth century. The nation was now somewhat belatedly ready to take its part in a competitive struggle which was to demand an increasing degree of technical knowledge and skill not only from the leaders but also from the rank and file. The beginning of a national system of technical education lies in the Act of 1889, to be carried out under central supervision by the county and county borough councils set up in the previous year (the former for the country, the latter for the large towns). It remained for the great Education Act of 1902 to make these councils responsible for all secondary education, which was then rapidly developed. This Act abolished the old school boards and also handed elementary education over to the councils. One effect of this change was that part of the rates levied by the councils

---

[1] Hamilton Fyffe, *Northcliffe* (Allen & Unwin, 1930). Lord Morley called the *Daily Express* a 'huge engine for keeping discussion at a low level'. At a later date Sir Harold Nicolson remarked that Northcliffe's papers were aimed 'not at the thoughts of their countrymen but at their emotions'.

was now used for the teaching of Church of England tenets to which the Nonconformists objected. Their refusal to pay rates was the first of the series of revolts against the State which we shall trace in their increasing violence in the next chapter. The Act of 1902 was a Conservative measure: there were over a hundred Nonconformist M.P.s in the Liberal majority of 1906, for the Nonconformist conscience was one of the great forces of the time and could not be outraged with impunity.

The Conservatives had been in power for a generation before this book begins: from 1886, with an interval from 1892–5, until December 1905. The governments of that period were still largely aristocratic.[1] In Lord Salisbury's original Cabinet of 1886 the Prime Minister, the Chancellor of the Exchequer, the Foreign Secretary, the First Lord of the Admiralty, the President of the Board of Trade and five other Cabinet Ministers were peers. In fact, only four out of fourteen members of the Cabinet were in and could therefore debate and be questioned in the House of Commons. Even in Lord Rosebery's Liberal Cabinet of 1894 the Foreign Secretary as well as the Prime Minister and four other members were in the House of Lords—an arrangement which would have been considered intolerable even fifteen years later. Lord Salisbury indeed, while for five years both Prime Minister and Foreign Secretary, seldom consulted his colleagues on foreign affairs and generally conducted his skilful diplomacy in private letters to his ambassadors, written in his own hand in the library of Hatfield House—the home of his ancestors who had served Queen Elizabeth I. In the first Parliament of Edward VII's reign— the first of which Mr. Winston Churchill was a member—Lord Salisbury was Prime Minister, his nephew Arthur Balfour, Leader of the House of Commons, another nephew and a cousin were members of the Cabinet, a son and another relative were in the Government.

Although government still lay in the hands of the great aristo- cratic families up to 1906, the landed gentry had been hard hit by the decline in agriculture, and the last decades of Victoria's reign are marked by the 'arrival' of the commercial, suburban

[1] From 1832–67 every Prime Minister except Peel belonged to the landed aristocracy, as did most of his colleagues.

middle classes. It is to them that the Edwardians–and we, and the world–owe our inheritance of games. The old landed society *did not play games*. Its recreations were hunting, fishing, shooting and horse-racing. Organised games–football, cricket and tennis–must be played at a centre, easily reached by the city dweller, whether as player or spectator. The rules of association football were drawn up in 1863; the English Rugby Union was founded in 1871, and the game of tennis was patented in 1874. Golf, played time without mind in Scotland, did not become popular in England until after 1885. So recent is this part of the inheritance bequeathed by the Victorian middle classes to their Edwardian successors.

Yet it was aristocratic governments (one Tory, one Liberal) which in 1867 and 1884 gave the vote to a large proportion of adult men, and thus made the election of Members of Parliament substantially democratic.[1] This is perhaps the most important part of the Edwardian heritage, for over 6,700,000 men could vote, yet there were only 10,000 incomes above £13 weekly and 900,000 between £3 and £13. The remainder of the 40,000,000 of the population drew less than £3 a week. The vote was bound be used to make living conditions more uniform–in other words, to bring about great social changes. They took some time to come, and for a generation after 1884 the governing classes were unshaken. Yet the new electorate threw up its own new party. The Labour Representation Committee was formed in 1900 with Ramsay MacDonald as its secretary. Nineteen hundred and six saw the birth of the Labour Party and the new House of Commons of that year contained twenty-nine Labour members and twenty-three miners' representatives. Ignoring, if one can, the Irish Nationalists, there were now three parties where historically there had been two and in a political system which tends towards two.

A new society was now striving to be born.

---

[1] They were soon to vote themselves a salary, thus making it possible for men without private means or trade-union posts to become members.

3

'The Seething and Teeming'

1909–1914[1]

'THE sudden realisation of a changing world which burst on the nation in 1906 was breathtaking. The good, easy man of 1901 may be compared with the comfortable citizen of the *pays-bas*, living his ordered life in his tidy house behind the great dykes. For years he had been aware of tides and murmurs. Little gaps had sprung in the dykes, but the wardens had repaired them and kept the barrier in good order. A trickle or two had seeped through, doing no great damage, even stimulating the comfortable sense of security and smugness behind the walls. And then a day came when suddenly the tide rose higher, the waves beat more strongly, the gaps increased in size and number, the wardens could no longer cope with them, and panic reports began to filter in with the sea. The wall was giving, the sea encroaching, and the threat to snug security and tidiness and old-established ways was a reality. In the middle of the reign of Edward VII, Victorianism formally died and the era of war and revolution began. And this violent change, this sharp division between two epochs, came on the bulk of the nation like a thief in the night. At home and abroad it seemed that every pent force was obeying a common impulse to break out. The Victorian dyke could stand the strain no longer.'[2]

What was it that happened in 1906? There was a Liberal Government after, apart from one brief interval, twenty years—

---

[1] 'The seething and teeming of this pre-war period, its immense ferment and its restless fertility'–R. C. K. Ensor, *op. cit.*

[2] John Gore, *op. cit.*

that is a generation—of Tory rule. Moreover, the Liberals came in with a resounding majority of eighty-four over all the other parties combined. But however large their majority in the House of Commons, they faced a permanently and overwhelmingly Tory House of Lords, with unrestricted power to amend and to reject their dearest legislation. Thus was precipitated that great conflict between the Commons and the Lords, one of the most dramatic in modern British history.

It is difficult for us, we who have seen the Russian royal family murdered, Hitler dictator over Germany, thrones, dynasties and aristocracies swept away, to realise the true horror with which Lord Lansdowne (the leader of the House of Lords), Lord Willoughby de Broke, Lord Hugh Cecil, and the good Tories of 1908 saw the Radical Lloyd George assume office as Chancellor of the Exchequer. We must beware of looking at events through our eyes instead of theirs, and of wrongly adjudging them hypocrites. To Lord Salisbury's sons, to the 'backwoodsmen' peers, to Salisbury's nephew Balfour, now leader of the Opposition, it was almost beyond the limits of reason that the orphan son of a village schoolmaster, brought up by a shoemaker uncle, should become a Cabinet Minister.[1]

Since 1895 the Lords had allowed their power of revising legislation passed on from the Commons to lie dormant. Now they became a permanent Opposition—became, as Mr. Lloyd George put it, 'Mr. Balfour's poodle'. In 1906 they killed the Liberals' Education Bill (the Bill to revise the Education Act of 1902, which had so outraged the Nonconformists that it greatly helped the Liberals to power). In the same year a Bill to abolish the second vote enjoyed by some businessmen was also killed, and in 1907 four land-reform Bills were either mutilated or rejected. Some of these were indeed partisan measures and the Education Act of 1902 has proved worth preserving. But in 1908 the Lords were unquestionably wrong to support the liquor trade by rejecting a Licensing Bill intended to reduce what was then the monstrous evil of drunkenness. This was no party measure

---

[1] Nor, of course, did Lloyd George intend to endear himself to them with such remarks as: 'A fully-equipped duke costs as much to keep up as two Dreadnoughts, and dukes are just as great a terror and they last longer.'

and King Edward urged on Lord Lansdowne that it would be impolitic to reject it.

In 1909 Lloyd George introduced what he called his 'People's Budget'–a Budget intended to raise the money with which to pay for the Liberal Government's old-age pensions and for increased expenditure on the Navy (but one which left the maximum rate of super-tax at 1s. 8d. in the pound as against to-day's 10s.). The Lords rejected the Budget. This made a general election in 1910 inevitable–and the issue put to the voters was inevitably the functions and the future of the House of Lords. The Liberals were returned, and on 14th April 1910 the Parliament Bill was introduced, with the intention of securing the ultimate supremacy of the Commons over the Lords. Three weeks later King Edward died suddenly and George V succeeded to the throne. The further stages of the Parliament Bill were postponed; it was hoped that some way might still be found to save him also succeeding to a great constitutional crisis.

As briefly as possible we have set the political scene for the drama of the Parliament Act which was to be played to its end in the stifling summer of 1911. Before we start our chronological account of the events of those tense years from 1910 until the final curtain fell in August 1914 we must hastily paint in three more backcloths–those of the struggles of organised labour, of the Irish Problem, and of the suffragettes–for the Liberal Ministers were bedevilled by them all.

The war waged against the State by the extremist suffragettes is probably unique in history. The movement was primarily middle-class, for the change to smaller families towards the end of the nineteenth century gave middle-class wives more leisure. Moreover, large numbers of men from the upper and middle classes were occupied abroad in the administration of Empire and this left a number of women at home unmarried but leisured, for few paid employments were then open to them and it was customary that their families should support them.

Women already had the vote in Australia, New Zealand and Finland. In 1907 they qualified for election as county and borough councillors and were already available as Poor Law guardians and members of education committees. After the Married Women's

Property Acts of 1887 and 1893 a woman was no longer obliged to hand her personal fortune meekly to her husband on marriage, and in 1891 the courts significantly ruled that a husband cannot legally detain his wife in his house. Women were entering offices and had just begun their penetration of higher education and the professions. Their Victorian banishment from public affairs was already challenged. But they had not got the vote.

Bills for the enfranchisement of women had been introduced and as regularly shelved for thirty years before the issue became a live one with the arrival of the Liberal Government. Although it was not a party issue, some members of both parties being for and some against, the Women's Social and Political Union reasoned that only the Government could grant the vote and it was only the Government they attacked. The founder and head of the W.S.P.U. was that intense human flame Emmeline Pankhurst, mother of the round-faced Christabel and of Sylvia, and widow of a middle-class leader of the Independent Labour Party. With the great and complementary abilities of Emmeline Pankhurst and Mrs. Emmeline Pethick-Lawrence the movement progressed steadily from 1906 until the autumn of 1912. Under the increasing influence of Christabel–who escaped imprisonment and the obscenities of forced feeding by living in Paris, where she was visited secretly by devoted couriers–the movement became somewhat snobbish and extremely autocratic, although the branch under Sylvia Pankhurst remained socialist and more realistic. But Sylvia was expelled from the W.S.P.U. by her sister.

The decision to intensify militancy after July 1912 was that of Christabel, using her influence over her mother. It was this belligerence which probably prevented the passing of some kind of Women's Suffrage Bill between 1906 and 1914; yet, strangely enough, the political unwisdom of violence became almost irrelevant in the end to many of the women. 'The means mattered rather than the end and conflicted with it.'[1] They were possessed by a strange rapture; the vote was sought less for any practical use than as a *symbol* of equality: ultimately it went almost further;

[1] Ensor, *op. cit.*

there was a withdrawal from the world of men as from a con-
tact which sullied and debased the purity of English woman-
hood.

Suffragette militancy was a revolt against the conventions of
society, an attack on organised social life. It was a refusal to play
the game according to the rules, and to this refusal a democratic
government, depending on the consent of the governed, is
peculiarly vulnerable. The years 1906 to 1914 saw a crescendo
of such rule-breaking. Minorities were unwilling to accept majority decisions, and majorities to avoid outraging the feelings of
minorities.

It was after 1910 that the trade unions, fighting for recognition
by the employers, for the first time challenged the State. These
were no longer craft unions, but were already organised on the
basis of one great union for each great industry. It was a period
also in which real wages were slightly falling—notably after 1910—
after an unbroken and rapid rise for fifty years.[1] Social reform of
the Lloyd George stamp, moreover, did not satisfy them, for his
insurance scheme demanded contributions from the workers.
Syndicalism was spreading from France and remained a strong
influence in the unions until 'direct action' was proved ineffective
by the end of 1912 and the unions again turned to parliamentary
methods: the syndicalists favoured direct action for influencing
Parliament from outside, instead of attempting to capture it from
inside; that is the lightning strike, the stay-in strike, the sym-
pathetic strike, sabotage and the general strike.

It is difficult for us to-day to realise the extent to which the
Irish Problem—and it demands capitals—bedevilled British politics
while the Irish were still represented at Westminster. To a
generation which has witnessed the titanic and tragic upheaval
effected by the partition of India, and has seen the map of Europe
re-drawn and again re-drawn, Irish partition seems strangely
remote and its bitterness difficult to understand. Militant agitation for Irish Home Rule dates back to 1870 and is itself only
another—but more positive—version of the old demand for repeal

[1] Real wages—and the reader must be warned that the term is inescapable nowadays—
are taken to mean *what wages will buy*, after allowing for any fluctuations in the value of
the money in which they are expressed; i.e. an increase in money wages is not necessarily
an increase in real wages if each £1 buys less than it did.

of the Union. In 1877 Irish obstruction twice kept the Commons up all night—an unbelievable outrage.

The kernel of the problem, as it concerns us, is that Catholic, 'native' Southern Ireland wished to be independent of Britain, but Protestant, 'settler' Ulster insisted on its right to remain united with Britain for fear of becoming a permanent minority (although Belfast is a larger city than Dublin). Partition of Ireland's soil was anathema to good Irishmen of both parties.

Even as late as 1910 the English Tory Party—now calling themselves Unionists—might have persuaded the Ulstermen to accept a degree of local independence within an Irish state governed from Dublin. But the Tory Unionists were the Opposition at Westminster, and to embarrass the Liberals they went to unwise, even reprehensible lengths in strengthening Ulster opposition to being governed from Dublin. In 1910 Sir Edward Carson was invited to lead a group of Irish Unionists in the House of Commons, and this strange, masterful man increasingly imposed his will upon his English colleagues. The Liberals, too, however, in the later stages of their bitter struggle with the Tories or Unionists over the House of Lords, were dependent on Irish votes, and Irish votes depended on the Home Rule Bill, which the Liberal Government laid before the Commons in 1912, and which was intended to give limited self-government to a single Irish Parliament.

The scene is set. The drama moves towards the tragedy of war.

On 16th June 1910 a round-table conference on parliamentary reform called by King George V met at 10 Downing Street, but failed to reach agreement. On 1st September the Ely Pit in South Wales was closed and its 900 miners thrown out of work. By 1st November all the men in the Rhondda Valley were on strike. Between 12th and 21st rioting increased and a mobile force of 1,400 constabulary, 200 cavalry picking their way carefully on the icy roads, and two companies of infantry were sent into the valley. 'In Tonypandy some despairing police, slowly beaten down with nail-studded mandril sticks, pieces of iron and flints . . . were only rescued by Maj. Freeth and the Lancashire Fusiliers. Inspector Anderson, Capt. Lindsay (Chief Constable of Glamorgan), and the Metropolitan Police, charging up the cliff-like side streets of Pennycraig, were assailed from upper windows with flints, bricks, crockery, and chamber-pots.'[1] Not until 1st August of the following year were the miners starved back to work.

While this was going on Mr. Asquith was in the midst of his battle with the Lords. No agreement had been reached. If the Parliament Bill was to be passed by the House of Lords it could only be forced through by creating enough new Liberal peers to swamp the Tories. The King could not contemplate such a massive creation of peers without a fresh reference to the electorate, a second general election in 1910. On 18th November 1910, with the election not a month away (and much of the Metropolitan Police deployed with the Lancashire Fusiliers in the Rhondda), the House of Commons was besieged by the suffragettes, demonstrating against the Government's apparent refusal to find ways and means of passing the so-called Conciliation Bill, which would have given the vote to about a million women. The Home Secretary, Mr. Winston Churchill, had given orders that the women were to be kept away from the Houses of Parliament. When the perspiring police were goaded beyond endurance by a strange sort of passive resistance: 'Bannerettes were torn and trampled; women were struck with fists and knees, knocked down, dragged up, hurled from hand to hand, and sent reeling back, bruised and bleeding, into the arms of the crowd . . . they were pummelled and they were pinched, their thumbs were forced back, their arms twisted . . . their faces rubbed against the palings: and this went on for nearly six hours . . . the battle ended at last by lamplight. The Square was cleared. By the wall of the House of Lords a number of anxious women kneeled around Miss Ada Wright, who had been knocked down a dozen times in succession, and was in a very bad way. A few torn bannerettes, a trampled hat or two, some fragments of clothing remained on the field of battle until next morning. . . .'[2] It was the suffragettes' Black Friday.

Three days later Mrs. Emmeline Pethick-Lawrence led a

---

[1] G. Dangerfield, *The Strange Death of Liberal England* (Constable, 1936). What this chapter owes to Mr. Dangerfield's book will be obvious even to those who do not know it. It should be added that the South Wales strike was by no means the first of the year.

[2] Dangerfield, *op. cit.*

raiding party which demonstrated that the spirit of militarism was not broken. Concealing stones and hammers in their hand-bags, her party shattered the windows of the Home Office, the War Office, the Foreign Office, the Board of Education, the Board of Trade, the Treasury, Somerset House, the National Liberal Club, several post offices, the Old Banqueting Hall, the London and S.W. Bank, the houses of Mr. Haldane, War Secretary, and of Mr. John Burns, President of the Local Government Board.

In December the general election took place after fifteen months in which the issue of Lords *versus* the elected Commons had been constantly before the people. The new House of Commons returned in January 1911 consisted of 272 Liberals, 272 Unionists, 42 Labour and 80 Irish Nationalists–the last two giving the Liberals their majority, as in the previous Parliament. The Parliament Bill was passed by the Commons in May. Between the end of May and 6th July it was debated in the Lords–and it became surprisingly, inescapably certain that their lordships were going to fight. During this momentous debate, on 14th June, a general strike of seamen and firemen broke out at Southampton, followed on the 16th by a similar strike at Goole and on the 20th at Hull, where there was incendiarism, looting and riot. On 22nd June 1911 George V was solemnly crowned in Westminster Abbey.

It is necessary here to examine the international situation, which could never be far from the Liberal Ministers' thoughts as the maintenance of 'the hundred years peace' became increasingly precarious (that is, the hundred years, from 1815 to 1914, during which Britain was mercifully spared being involved in any major European war). Russia's quest for an ocean port which would not be frozen in winter was immemorial. She concentrated now on seeking it at what was anyhow her most convenient point, the Bosphorus and Dardanelles. 'Freedom of the Straits' under a weak Turkey was her immediate object; her method was to dominate the Balkan peninsula through its Slav populations.

But the decrepit bulk of the Austro-Hungarian dual monarchy lay across her flank. There was thus a primary conflict between

Russia and Austria-Hungary, with the latter mainly on the defensive, her policy being to maintain Turkey as a defence against Russia and the Slavs generally. It was Austria's concern to keep the Balkan states small and weak, for fear of their tearing lumps out of her—as indeed they did after she had lost the war. Austria-Hungary contained more Serbs than the kingdom of Serbia itself; her policy then was to keep Serbia small and unimportant, if possible to suppress Serbia altogether.

Germany's one firm ally in Europe was now Austria, whom she could not afford to abandon. Such was the pass to which her leaders had brought her after Bismarck's dismissal. Moreover, Germany nourished the ambition of creating an unbroken sphere of German influence from the Baltic down to the Persian Gulf. 'The conflict between the two thrusts—the Russian north to south and the German west to east—was absolute. And it needs to be clearly grasped, because it was what motived the war of 1914.'[1]

If there was war, France would be drawn in under the terms of the Dual Alliance, her treaty with Russia, which was officially acknowledged in 1896. Her participation would at once have raised in England the traditional question of the safety of the Channel ports, even if the entente between Britain and France had not been signed in 1904. Moreover, Germany had challenged Britain at sea. Control of the oceans was essential to British trade, and the British Empire could not accept Germany—the one power which challenged her at sea—as mistress of the European continent.

The instability of the Kaiser's temperament, his freedom from constitutional restraint and the malign professional influence of the German General Staff were factors which made a peaceful settlement more difficult. Already in 1905 he had precipitated a crisis at Tangier, and the Liberal Ministers, on taking the seals of office, were surprised and distressed to learn how uncertain was the international situation. In 1908 there was another crisis, and now in July 1911 the German gunboat H.I.M.S. *Panther* lay off Agadir, brusquely intent on securing Germany compensation for any extension of French interests in Morocco. On 3rd July

[1] Ensor, *op. cit.*, on which this analysis is based.

Sir Edward Grey, the Foreign Secretary, told the German Ambassador that the situation must be discussed at a meeting of the British Cabinet. The following day he conveyed the Cabinet's decision that Britain would not recognise any new arrangements made without her. For seventeen anxious days there was no reply from Germany, while the German fleet was steaming off the coast of Norway, well placed for a sudden attack across the North Sea and preparations were also made on our side: 'the Admiralty wireless whispers through the ether to the tall masts of ships', as Mr. Churchill put it.

On 21st July Mr. Lloyd George was due to speak at the Mansion House in the City of London. In this now historic speech the Chancellor of the Exchequer asserted that Britain, if she felt her interests endangered, would fight. It was a tense moment. Germany was enraged, but the effect of the speech was enhanced by the person of the speaker, for Lloyd George was known as a Radical and a Germanophile and it had been felt that he might split the Cabinet on this issue. Meanwhile the struggle over the Parliament Bill continued with increasing personal bitterness, and on 24th July the Prime Minister was howled down in the House of Commons by the Unionists in a scene then utterly without precedent.

The following day Sir Edward Grey warned the Admiralty that the fleet might be attacked at any moment. On 1st August of that stifling summer, the hottest in seventy years, a dockers' strike started in London and on 5th August a carters' strike broke out in Liverpool. On 7th August the Mayor of Liverpool was obliged to ask the Home Office for the help of the military. Next day the London carman's trade union came out. The stoppage in London lasted until 11th August—meanwhile Europe's royalty was arriving to witness the splendour of the coronation naval review at Cowes. 'Slowly on London came down that unreal Sabbath quiet—"when the great markets by the sea shut fast"'.

'Everything began to die—coal and water service, gas and electricity, railway, road and river transport. Vegetables and flour grew scarcer and scarcer; great piles of fruit lay perishing in the docks. As for the butter trade, the Danish butter came in casks and was not refrigerated: it was growing rancid in the mounting heat. The frozen meat from Argentina, the United States, and New Zealand–on which the city largely depended–was going bad, for there was a shortage of cold-storage accommodation, and the refrigerating ships themselves lay useless in the river without coal. Famine drew nearer hour by hour, the strike had spread out to Brentford and the Medway. It seemed as if the whole Thames Valley must shortly be affected.'[1]

Nerves were taut, as they are when the weather is breathless, particularly the nerves of the dockers awake at night in the stifling slums of the East End of 1911. But other nerves were equally stretched–namely those of the Lords, whose debate on the Parliament Bill was adjourned on 9th August with its outcome still unpredictable. Against the unnatural stillness of strike-bound London, the debate in the House of Lords entered its final stage at 4.30 p.m. on 10th August, with the temperature 97° in the shade. Its drama has rarely been surpassed in Parliament, as speaker followed speaker passionately determined to sway the minds of the assembled peers, many of them 'backwoodsmen', drawn from their country houses for their votes and seldom if ever previously seen within the precincts of the House of Lords. On the one hand Lord Lansdowne and the more moderate Unionist leaders unwillingly counselled withdrawal; on the other side there was a blind determination to 'die in the last ditch' under the leadership of Lord Halsbury and Lord Willoughby de Broke.[2] The great constitutional issue which had been pending and becoming more acute since 1906 remained undecided, the result unpredictable, until the final division at 10.45 p.m., when it was seen that the Parliament Act had passed.[3]

By 14th August, in spite of the police, the Scots Greys, the Warwickshire Regiment and a small committee sent by the

[1] Dangerfield, *op. cit.*
[2] Who described it as ' . . . legislation which is not only extraordinary but in our view absolutely unthinkable and impossible'.
[3] Its first clause provides that a Money Bill passes into law over the Lords' veto after a delay of one month, but the definition of a Money Bill is narrow and no great number of Bills have been so certified.

Its second clause, by which other Bills may be passed despite the Lords' veto after a delay of two years, has been fully used only three times: for the Home Rule Bill and the Welsh Church Disestablishment Bill, which both became law (ineffectively) in 1914, and in 1947 for another Parliament Bill by which Mr. Attlee's Labour Government reduced the period of delay to one year.

Labour Party, rioting was so frequent that the Liverpool ship-owners declared a lock-out of all men engaged on handling cargo. In return, all the city's transport workers struck. By the following day it was clear that the railwaymen throughout the country wanted a general stoppage. This was no step initiated by the executives of the four railway unions; it was a spontaneous movement from below, which the executives could only control by accepting. Meeting hurriedly in Liverpool, they issued an ultimatum to the railway companies demanding recognition of the unions within twenty-four hours.

On 17th August Mr. Asquith offered a Royal Commission to enquire into the unions' demands. This was curtly refused, to the deep chagrin of the Prime Minister, who was stung to make the remark: 'Then your blood be upon your own head.' By 18th August the country's railways within an area bounded by New-castle, Hull, Coventry and Liverpool were almost at a standstill. Industrial England was paralysed. Troops were despatched to twenty-seven different centres; troops camped in the London parks. London indeed was an armed camp and every regiment in England was mobilised at full strength. By 19th August, apart from the London and S.W. Railway, there were only a few trains on the move, crawling with difficulty from point to point.

The greater crisis resolved the lesser. Lloyd George successfully brought about a settlement, pending the report of a Royal Commission, by an appeal for national unity in face of the menace from abroad. Between 8th and 22nd September the tunnels and bridges of the South-Eastern Railway were patrolled day and night, for fear lest sabotage should interrupt a line which might at any moment become vitally important. The Agadir Crisis lasted until 11th October, when a Morocco Accord was signed by the powers.

Industrial unrest broke out again in the spring of 1912, and on 1st March the miners—and significantly this was a national movement—struck for a minimum wage of 5s. a shift for men and 2s. for boys. About 850,000 men were out and the Government intervened. (To our generation the intervention of government in industrial disputes has become commonplace, but it was then an innovation.) After four agonised days of conference Mr.

Asquith was obliged to admit his inability to reconcile the ob-
duracy of the coal-owners with the determination of the miners.
Meanwhile–as during the winter of 1947–'industry all over the
country began to limp, to hesitate and to shut down'. The process
continued: towards the end of the month the iron and steel,
glass, pottery and brick-making industries were nearly idle, the
railways jerking to a standstill, the paralysis spreading to fishing
and the ports.

Something else also happened on 1st March: '. . . little groups
of women, expensively dressed and carrying large but fashionable
bags, drifted with perfect nonchalance into the West End. Picca-
dilly and the Haymarket first resounded with the smashing of
glass; thither rushed police and pedestrians, and women with
hammers in their hands . . . were the centre of little groups,
which accompanied them, in considerable excitement, all the
way to the police station. But scarcely had the last offender been
bundled safely inside, when, once again, the sound of ruined glass
splintered the evening air. This time it was Regent Street and
the Strand which suffered. The police hurried off to these new
scenes of destruction, and no sooner had they rounded up the
culprits than the windows of Oxford Circus and Bond Street
crashed in their ears. Upon that crowded and brilliantly lighted
quarter there descended a rattling darkness, as shutters were
fixed and iron curtains came down on the run. . . . But all these
precautions were in vain. The tactic of ruining in relays worked
perfectly, and the ordered destruction went on until half-past
six. Lyons and Appenrodts, the great shipping firms in Cockspur
Street, Cook's, the Kodak Company, Swan and Edgar, Marshall
and Snelgrove, Jay's, Liberty's, Fuller's, Swears and Wells, Hope
Brothers, the Carrara Marble Works–these, and other famous
businesses, were visited by the relentless hammer, until the
damage had mounted into thousands of pounds.

'Meanwhile the indomitable Mrs. Pankhurst had driven off in
a taxi to Downing Street, where, at half-past five exactly, she and
two colleagues succeeded in throwing four stones through the
Prime Minister's windows and disappeared, hustled but triumphant, within the portals of Cannon Row police station.'[1]

[1] Dangerfield, *op. cit.*

On 4th March 3,000 police converged on Parliament Square, where they had been led to expect a demonstration. But they were outmanœuvred. They waited in vain, while almost every window in Knightsbridge was smashed. VOTES FOR WOMEN was burned in acid in the smooth green of golf-links; at least two of some women bold enough to heckle Mr. Lloyd George in Wales were reduced to absolute nudity; castles and churches were set on fire, pictures slashed, windows shattered. For the cause, delicately nurtured women allowed themselves to be hustled by crowds, endured imprisonment and regularly staged hunger-strikes, although they knew this would involve the degrading performance of forcible feeding through a tube.

On 15th March Mr. Asquith announced his intention to terminate the miners' strike by an Act of Parliament setting up machinery for the negotiation of a minimum wage. The Prime Minister said, 'I speak under the stress of very strong feeling. We have exhausted all our powers of persuasion and argument and negotiation.' It appeared to his audience that the Prime Minister himself had reached a state of nervous exhaustion. The Act, which was pushed through the Lords with some difficulty, became law on 29th March and proved successful, but the Government had been unable to bring about a settlement between groups within the State by any other means.

On 21st May all the lightermen in the Port of London were out on strike again, and by the 23rd the movement had spread to most of the transport workers in London and on the Medway. Mr. Asquith was on holiday; Mr. Lloyd George and other Ministers intervened. A body representing the employers replied: 'The employers desire that it should be distinctly understood that whilst they are willing to discuss with His Majesty's Ministers at all times any suggestions made by them, no such suggestions, however acceptable in other respects, will be adopted until work is resumed throughout the Port.' As indeed it was, for the other ports would not co-operate with the London dockers, funds were low after the great strikes of the previous year, and by 6th August the London dockers had been starved back to work.

The year drew towards its close with the declaration of war by Bulgaria, Greece, Serbia and Montenegro on Turkey, who was barely able to stop their armies outside Constantinople. Sir Edward Grey called a conference of ambassadors which met in London under his chairmanship in December. On 16th December peace delegates from the warring states also met in London and the two conferences continued alongside each other until near the end of January 1913. After a resumption of fighting the Balkan War was ended by a treaty of peace signed in London at the end of May.

In March 1913 Bills were submitted to the German Reichstag which, at any rate in the lurid light of subsequent events, resemble preparations for war between the two alliances of Great Powers. On 26th March Mr. Churchill, now First Lord of the Admiralty, unsuccessfully proposed a naval building 'holiday' to Germany. On 4th June Emily Davison, ecstatic devotee of women's suffrage and faithful admirer of Christabel Pankhurst, sacrificed her life for the cause by throwing herself in front of the King's horse at the Derby. At the end of that month the Second Balkan War broke out with a Bulgarian offensive against Serbia and Greece and a precarious peace was not restored until 10th August.

Nor was lawlessness confined to 'foreigners', to women or to the struggles of workmen on strike. We must note that on 12th July Mr. Bonar Law, now leader of the Unionist Opposition, sent a message to Sir Edward Carson in Ulster: 'Whatever steps you may feel compelled to take, whether they are constitutional, or whether in the long run they are unconstitutional, you have the whole Unionist Party, under my leadership, behind you.' The Irish crisis had indeed reached a pitch at which London was filled with rumours that the King intended to abdicate—rumours which showed how little the intense devotion to duty of King George V was then understood.

On 26th August, under Jim Larkin's leadership, there began the great Dublin transport strike which closed the port and remained unsettled until early December. One of its indirect effects was to create the industrial Triple Alliance of the National Union of Railwaymen, the Miners' Federation of Great Britain and the National Transport Workers' Federation, whose leaders became aware how much more effectively the cause of each could be advanced if all three acted together. On 18th October Mr. Churchill repeated to Germany his offer of a cessation of rivalry in naval building, again without success. The following month in Dublin Mr. Bonar Law–having previously stated that the power of the Liberal Government was usurped–went on to invite the Army not to obey it.

In March 1914, for the first time since the year 1688 in the reign of King James II, the Government of the day found itself in fact unable to rely on the Army carrying out its orders. The incident is known as the Mutiny at the Curragh and its significance was lost neither on the Germans nor on the French, each of whom saw it with very different feelings. By now the Ulstermen, led by Sir Edward Carson, backed by the Unionists and possessing their own well-drilled militia or private army, were almost beyond control. Mr. Churchill despatched the Third Battle Squadron, together with eight destroyers of the Fourth Flotilla and H.M. ships *Pathfinder* and *Attentive*, to Belfast Lough– a show of strength such as the Royal Navy had not hitherto been called upon to display against its own nationals. Throughout much of 18th March General Paget, Commander-in-Chief Ireland, was pleading, not unsuccessfully, with Colonel Seely, the Secretary for War, for some concession to those officers who felt unable, owing to their political sympathies, to operate against the Ulster Volunteers. Next day he telegraphed from Dublin: 'Officer Commanding 5th Lancers states that all officers except two, and one doubtful, are resigning their commissions to-day. I much fear same conditions in the 16th Lancers. Fear men will refuse to move.' And again: 'Regret to report Brigadier and 57 officers Third Cavalry Brigade prefer to accept dismissal if ordered North.' In London, Sir Henry Wilson, Director of Military Operations, suggested to his intimates that the screws should now be put on 'Asquith and his crowd'.

The storm of resentment against this treasonable behaviour broke in Parliament on 25th March. Seely and Generals French and Ewart resigned, Asquith became Minister for War as well as Prime Minister. But the storm was purely parliamentary–no drastic action followed in Ireland. A month later indeed the s.s. *Fanny* landed some 30,000 rifles and bayonets at Larne–a serious

1. The English country house at the turn of the century—the staff, with the housekeeper in the centre, flanked by the coachman and head keeper.

2. A middle-class interior, 1902.

3. 1912: working-class school-children setting off for a day in the country.

Picture Post Lib.

addition to the 5,000 or 6,000 which the Ulster Volunteers already possessed. On 21st May the Home Rule Bill came up for its third reading in the Commons and was shouted down by the Opposition. The Liberals and Unionists were no longer on speaking terms, their leaders communicating through liaison officers. Lord Curzon even gave a ball which the King and Queen attended, but to which the Prime Minister and Mrs. Asquith were not invited!

Nor was there any sign of lessened irritability in the industrial field. Between January and July of 1914 there were no less than 937 strikes. Everything, in fact, pointed to 1914 as the year in which the community would for the first time in its history be faced with a general strike. There were a number of factors all operating in the one direction. The Trade Unions Act of the previous year gave the unions a great measure of legal indemnity. The industrial Triple Alliance gave them considerable confidence of success. Each of the three great unions of the alliance was discontented: the miners because their great strike of 1912 had only established a minimum wage in principle; in practice they were not generally getting the 5s. and 2s. In October 1913, moreover, 439 lives were lost in a terrible explosion in the Senghenydd mine—the manager of which was subsequently fined the sum of £22 for having failed to observe Home Office safety regulations. The railwaymen were dissatisfied because, despite the virtual recognition of their unions resulting from the strike of 1911, the railway companies were victimising trade-union members. The third member of the alliance, the National Transport Workers' Federation, still resented the failure of the London transport strike of 1912, which its lack of funds had made it unable to support. By July there were disputes in the London building and electrical trades; the Marine Engineers' Union was demanding an eight-hour day; the engineers and boilermakers were in dispute with the Great Western Railway, and the General Labourers' Union was campaigning for improved conditions.

Between the end of May and the beginning of June the American Colonel House—confidential emissary of President Wilson—formed the opinion that the military families were in control in Berlin and had determined that the time was come for war.

D

On 4th July the munition workers of Woolwich Arsenal all downed tools over the dismissal of a single man.

In the same first seven months of 1914 107 buildings were fired by the suffragettes. Between 9th March and 18th July Mrs. Pankhurst was imprisoned four more times and endured four more hunger-strikes.

On 28th June 1914 the heir to the throne of Austria-Hungary was assassinated at Serajevo in Serbia. On 5th July the Kaiser promised the aged Austrian emperor Germany's full support in his action against Serbia. On 21st July King George V personally opened at Buckingham Palace the second conference called during the four years of his reign between Government and Opposition— a conference on the future of Ulster which broke up in failure on the 24th. There seemed to remain no alternative to civil war between the Irish Nationalists and the Ulster Volunteers under the Provisional Government which Sir Edward Carson had established in Belfast. But before the conference broke up the Austrian ultimatum had already been presented to Serbia.

The British Cabinet spent all the afternoon of 24th July discussing Ulster. It was about to separate, wrote Mr. Churchill, '. . . when the quiet grave tones of Sir Edward Grey's voice were heard, reading a document which had just been brought him from the Foreign Office. It was the Austrian note to Serbia. He had been reading or speaking for several minutes before I could separate my mind from the tedious and bewildering debate which had just closed. We were all very tired, but gradually, as the sentences followed one another, impressions of a wholly different character began to form in my mind. This note was clearly an ultimatum; but it was an ultimatum such as had never been penned in modern times. As the reading proceeded it seemed absolutely impossible that any state in the world could accept it, or that any acceptance, however abject, would satisfy the aggressor. The parishes of Tyrone and Fermanagh faded back into the mists and squalls of Ireland, and a strange light began immediately, but by perceptible gradations, to fall and glow upon the map of Europe.'[1]

[1] Winston S. Churchill, *The World Crisis 1911–1918* (abridged and revised edition, 1931, Odhams Press Ltd.).

The war neither caused the internal tensions of the time nor, with the exception of woman's suffrage, did it resolve them. Instead it brusquely interrupted the natural course of social change. But the thunderous barrage and mass slaughter, the horror and bitter suffering of the Great War brought to an end the world which our grandparents knew.

4

The Carnage and the Peace:
the First World War

THE scale of our narrative now changes. Before the war importance could rightly be attached to the smashing of shop windows in Knightsbridge or to the illicit arming of a few thousand Ulstermen. But now we deal with cataclysmic events: with 60,000 British casualties in a day; with the collapse of the ancient Austro-Hungarian and Imperial Russian empires and the birth of six new states; the rise of a strange new form of government in the vast territories of Russia; the reduction of Germany's currency to a heap of valueless paper. From 1914 on the pressure of great events continues almost without abatement until to-day, gaining only since 1939 in magnitude and intensity.

War to the soldier is 'the sensation of taking a profitless part in a game played by monkeys and organised by lunatics'.[1] It is not our task to trace the First World War in any detail, but we examine briefly the three main periods into which it falls. The first is marked by the onrush of the German armies almost to the gates of Paris. As by a miracle they were stopped on the River Marne and at least Field-Marshal von Moltke realised that with the loss of momentum they had lost the chance of decisively winning the war. Yet the cost to the French of stopping this first onslaught, in the first three months, was 854,000 men killed, wounded and prisoners; with the British

[1] Professor R. H. Tawney in *The Attack* (Allen & Unwin, 1952), which contains a moving autobiographical glimpse of what the Great War was like to the highly civilised soldier.

losses of 85,000 a total of 939,000 men against the German losses of 677,000 in the same period. One would expect the army which launches the attack against fortified positions to suffer more heavily than the defenders. That this was not so the French owed to their military thinkers' insistence on the doctrine that the best, almost the only means of defence is to attack, and to attack again and attack in all circumstances. It is necessary to insist on these and their later appalling losses, for they bled France white. They had their effect in 1939 when Mr. Churchill found that the pendulum had swung to the other extreme and that the French seemed unable to imagine the possibility of taking the offensive against the Germans. They had their effect between the two wars in France's passionate search for security against Germany; and they have their effect to-day.

But in 1914 the German armies were held at the Marne and the next three years witnessed the second phase–a deadlock on the Western Front. The trenches stretched from the sea in the north to neutral Switzerland in the south; there was no flank to turn. The Allied attack on the Dardanelles in 1915 was intended to throw Turkey out of the war and to turn the enemy's flank by permitting an attack through the Balkans on Austria-Hungary, but it failed. Neither side had sufficiently overwhelming superiority in men to break through the other's entrenched lines, nor had either side any effective method of attacking machine-guns and barbed wire.

That is not quite true. Early in the war the British Admiralty began to experiment with a fully enclosed armoured vehicle which could advance through mud by the use of caterpillar tracks and convey the men within it alive through the hail of bullets to the enemy trenches. There they could use the vehicle's own machine-guns with terrible effect. The vehicle was developed under the code name 'Tank' and the use of tanks was urged on the British High Command for two years before a good number of them were successfully employed in the British offensive at Cambrai in 1917. In a single day the whole German front line and all the supporting lines were completely penetrated on a maximum width of six miles. Ten thousand prisoners and 200 guns were captured for a loss of 1,500 British troops. The success could not be followed up, largely because no such success had been expected and no reserves were available to exploit it.

Yet tanks in insufficient numbers and on unsuitable ground had been foolishly revealed to the enemy in 1916 during the Battle of the Somme. It was fortunate that Hindenburg and Ludendorff were as blind to their revolutionary possibilities as were Sir John French and Sir Douglas Haig. Even after the war Lord Haig still gave it as his belief that, 'As time goes on, you will find just as much use for the horse, the well-bred horse, as you have ever done in the past'. As late as 1934 Mr. Duff Cooper, then Financial Secretary to the War Office, was still impressed 'by the importance of cavalry in modern warfare'. It is not unnatural that the British senior officers, cavalry and fox-hunting men themselves, had no wish to become 'garage mechanics', nor to assimilate such uncouth creatures into their messes. In effect, in 1923 the Royal Tank Corps had only four battalions and in 1933 it still had four battalions, equipped with the same type of tank. Despite their almost total uselessness in the previous war, the Army still maintained eighteen regiments of horsed cavalry. The recommendations of General Fuller in this country and of De Gaulle in France fell on the closed ears of those whose hopes still lay with the well-bred horse. Not so, however, in Germany, where Guderian developed the armoured division and the new mobile, mechanised warfare which went with it, so that when in 1940 the German Army next struck at France, with the aid of its dive-bombers it penetrated quickly to Paris and beyond Paris, seized the Channel ports, reached the Atlantic coast and subjugated the French people. They and their allies had little beyond naked courage to oppose at that time to the German armoured formations.

During the 'siege' warfare of 1915, 1916 and 1917 the commanders on both sides also had recourse to the naked courage of their soldiers. 'Good, plain, straightforward frontal attacks by valiant flesh and blood against wire and machine-guns.'[1] The anatomy of the attempts to break through the opposing lines was the same on both sides. A point of attack was selected: the Germans at Verdun chose the strongest of their enemies at his strongest point; the British on the Somme attacked what was then probably the most strongly fortified position in the world. Sur-

---

[1] Winston S. Churchill, *The World Crisis 1911-1918* (abridged and revised edition, Thornton Butterworth, 1931, now Odhams Press Ltd.).

prise was impossible, for an arterial system of railways and roads had first to be built to supply the selected battlefield. The area was then encircled by serried walls of cannon—when the French under black, bristling Mangin counter-attacked at Verdun in October 1916 and retook the fort of Douamont they had one gun to every fifteen yards of the enemy front. These guns demanded vast quantities of shells and mountainous supply dumps. When all was ready the stupendous barrage, continuing for days and nights, destroyed all life on the surface of the battlefield, but not the hardy defenders cowering in their underground dugouts. They emerged, when at last the barrage lifted, in time to mow down the attackers as they advanced through the unrecognisable chaos of the battlefield. At Passchendaele the guns destroyed the drainage of the Flanders fields and it happened that men and beasts advancing dumbly into the carnage were drowned in the mud.

Nor was much gained if the front were pierced, for the enemy could seal the breach more quickly than the ponderous apparatus of attack could be carried through it over the shattered ground. It was the theory that these repeated attacks would wear down the enemy's manpower—what was called the 'battle of attrition'. Now that we have the figures we know that in their offensives of 1916 and 1917 the British lost four officers to one German officer and nearly twice as many other ranks as the Germans. The Germans attacked Verdun on 21st February 1916 and by the end of April nearly a quarter of a million men from both sides had been killed and wounded in that place, without in any decisive way affecting the issue of the war. Even to-day Verdun is unlike any other place on earth. Little has grown where the subsoil has been brought up by the insensate fury of the shelling. Along the low ridge of the Mort Homme the solid earth has been whipped into shallow waves like the sea, and the movement of a man who tries to walk along it is like that of a boat breasting the waves. The few living inhabitants hardly break the silence maintained by the immense population of the dead, who are laid out on the hillsides in cemeteries like cities and whose spirits inhabit the sparse woodland, the forts and the trenches, were still visible in places after forty years.

Nineteen-seventeen saw unrestricted U-boat warfare and

Britain brought within sight of starvation, so great were the losses of our merchant ships on which supplies depended. Yet this desperate measure was the Germans' own undoing, for in April it induced the Americans to declare war–a few brief months before the Bolshevik Revolution led to the collapse of the Russian front and enabled the Germans to transport an additional million men to the West. In 1918, despite the arrival of the first American troops in France, the Germans broke through the Allied lines and resumed the onward surge which had been halted four years earlier. This marks the third period of the war, the final convulsion and the prelude to collapse. Between March and June 1918 the Germans lost 688,000 men in their great offensives. The generals, Haig, Joffre and Nivelle, Falkenhayn and Ludendorff destroyed not the forces of the enemy but their own armies.

The highest proportion of losses was suffered by the young officers, and it is not surprising to find that the number killed, counting the names which appear on the 1914–18 Roll of Honour of a boys' secondary school will usually be found to equal, more or less, the total number in the school at the beginning of the war.[1] Nor is it surprising that my generation grew up with a fear of arrogance and stupidity in generals which is lacking from my son's generation.[2] Indeed the comparative figures explain it:

	Killed or died of wounds in the war (excluding civilians)	
	1914–18	*1939–45*
British Empire[3]	1,104,890	359,372
France and her Colonies	nearly 1,500,000	250,000
Germany	,, 2,000,000	3,500,000

[1] G. A. N. Lowndes, *The Silent Social Revolution* (Oxford, 1937). In one school 720 old boys who were killed left only 80 sons behind them: it was the young subalterns whose casualties were highest.

[2] It is significant that the only aspect of our conduct of the Second War against which there has been some revulsion of feeling is the destruction of German cities and civilians by bombing, and this despite the acknowledged heroism of the R.A.F. aircrews who carried it out.

[3] The figure for 1914–18 is the final total reached by the Imperial War Graves Commission in 1933.

To end, as we began, with Tawney's words: 'From 1918 to 1939 the loathing of war was unquestionably the most powerful, the most general and the most constant of political emotions.' It was a cause of the Second World War.

Between 1914 and 1917 Russia lost nearly as many killed as all the Allies put together. The strain of the war brought about the collapse of the Czarist Government. In the midst of slaughter, defeat and famine the Czar was forced to abdicate in March 1917. A Provisional Government of Liberals was recognised by the Allies and endeavoured to continue the war. But–while the Germans, the Austrians and the Turks continued to batter on the cracking Russian fronts–deserting soldiers crowded the railways; supplies became increasingly disrupted; councils representing workmen and soldiers sprang up all over Russia. The Germans transported Lenin, the banished revolutionary, from Switzerland with Zinoviev in a sealed carriage and allowed them to pass across the front. They entered Petrograd (as Leningrad was then called) on 16th April and Trotsky joined them a month later. The struggle of the revolutionary councils or Soviets against the Provisional Government continued throughout October. On the night of 6th November Lenin and Trotsky felt themselves strong enough to seize power. With the aid of revolutionary troops and of the revolutionary sailors in the cruiser *Aurora*, anchored in the River Neva, the ineffective Liberal Government was thrown out. The Bolsheviks seized power and accepted the Germans' harsh terms for peace.

Russia under the Czars had been governed autocratically with the aid of the secret police; had imperialist dreams of expansion, but was backward, with a high proportion of illiterates and little industry. The bulk of the population were ignorant peasants, taught to revere the Czar as the Little Father of all the Russias. Under the Bolsheviks they were still governed autocratically, with the aid of a strengthened police and a body of fanatical Communists and informers, with the aid also of a greatly increased number of executions. The imperialist dreams might be postponed, but we have reason to know they were not forgotten. The people were taught to adulate first Lenin, then Stalin. More than half are still farmers, but it is a smaller proportion and by means of forced saving–at a rate impossible in peacetime in a free community–Russia has acquired a massive industry, second only to that of the United States. This great achievement has cost the Russian people more, probably many more, than 3 million lives lost through starvation and the executioner.

The efficient apparatus of modern dictatorship grips alike the peasants, organised into 'collective' farms, and the factory workers far more closely in their daily lives than could the ineffective government of the Czar. Only now, with the U.S.S.R. established as the second greatest military and industrial Power in the world, has the dictatorship been somewhat relaxed, first by Khrushchev, then by his successors. Now the Communist Party leaders are a little more attentive to the dissatisfaction of the peasants, to the people's demands for comfort and a higher standard of living. They vacillate between fear of falling behind the U.S.A. in force of arms and the desire to relax the tension under which their people have lived for so long.

Between the two world wars the U.S.S.R. came to stand–in wide circles outside the Communist Party–as the representative of the rights and interests of the working class throughout the world, as the champion of the underdog. The Communists appeared to have liberated the peasants, to have overthrown privilege and to have vindicated the common man. Warm feelings flowed out from the British working class to what seemed a great and promising social experiment. Friendship with Soviet Russia became almost an article of faith in the British Labour Party and to many Liberals; the Conservatives remained unwinkingly suspicious. This looking east to Russia for enlightenment despite her obvious material backwardness persisted in Labour and Liberal circles until the great Moscow trials of 1933 and the rising total of executions ('purges' is the modern term) made it quite plain that Communist Russia had no easy ideal to offer us. To those whose hopes betrayed their heads disillusionment was painful.

The Peace Conference which opened in Paris in January 1919 met against a background of famine and disease, of revolution, brigandage and civil war. The British public was impatient to see the peace treaty signed, the Kaiser hanged and the vast flow of German reparations which had been irresponsibly promised. The French, invaded by the Germans in 1870 and again in 1914, were boiling with anxiety about their future security. Italy had entered the war on the side of the Allies because that course promised to be the more profitable; her leaders were now pressing for the promised colonies and territorial gains at the expense of Austria. The Italians were a test case, for the principles maintained by President Wilson of the U.S.A. categorically excluded such old-world diplomatic huckstering. He had drawn up Fourteen Points, high-minded if somewhat vague principles on which the peace settlements were to be based. Yet behind him at home the opposition party in the U.S.A. was sarcastic about his scheme for reforming the world, calling loudly for the return of American troops and the repayment of American dollars. Moreover, the conference was originally planned—although in practice this proved impossible—to settle the affairs of the world before the eyes of the peoples of the world: 'We felt,' wrote Sir Harold Nicolson, 'like surgeons operating in the ballroom with the aunts of the patient gathered all around.'

The problem was not only to re-draw the map of Europe and much of Asia Minor, to determine the boundaries of the new states of Finland, Estonia, Latvia, Lithuania, Poland (revived after 150 years), Czechoslovakia, Yugoslavia, Irak, the French province of Syria and the British mandated territory of Palestine, the boundaries of France, Germany, Austria and Hungary. The main problem was the security of France. Mr. Churchill defined it with remarkable prescience when he wrote in 1929: 'How is a forty million France to be defended from invasion and destruction in the next generation against a sixty, seventy, eighty million Germany? There was the root problem of the Peace Conference . . . after 1940 Germany will have about twice as many men of military age as France.'[1]

This conference was also the first occasion on which the New World, the United States of America, emerged as a dominant power and bestrode the international stage. The enemy powers

[1] Winston S. Churchill, *The World Crisis, the Aftermath* (Butterworth, 1929).

were prostrate, the Allies at that time dependent on the U.S.A. for their food and finance. President Wilson decided to represent the U.S.A. personally in Paris. He was a professor, a lawyer, a devout Christian, convinced that in international affairs America was alone disinterested and possessed of a monopoly of rectitude. He had written: 'The United States have not the distinction of being masters of the world but the distinction of carrying certain lights for the world that the world has never so distinctly seen before, certain guiding lights of liberty and principle and justice.' On board the *George Washington*, three days before he landed triumphantly at Brest, he told his staff that the men with whom they were about to deal did not represent their peoples. 'The "dumb eyes of the people" haunted him with their mute, their personal appeal. He felt that these myriad eyes looked up to him as a prophet arisen in the West; as to a man chosen by God to give the whole world a new message and a more righteous order.'[1] In fact the boot was only too tragically on the other foot. The Prime Ministers of Britain, France and Italy–Lloyd George, Clemenceau the 'Tiger', and Orlando–represented only too well the emotions of their war-torn peoples. Wilson, however, was a bitter party politician and had failed to carry the United States Congress with him. His rival, ex-President Theodore Roosevelt, had already announced that 'Our allies and our enemies and Mr. Wilson himself should all understand that Mr. Wilson has no authority whatever to speak for the American people at this time'.

It is to the lasting honour of President Wilson's idealism that the Covenant of the League of Nations was written into the peace treaties and subscribed to by all the signatory countries. But beyond that is failure. European statesmen–anxious to make success appear less probable to an aggressor–were familiar with balanced alliances, strategic frontiers and armaments. President Wilson wished all this swept away in favour of a change of heart. If the U.S.A., with her decisive power, had backed this change of heart, as expressed in the League of Nations, then it was preferable to the checks and balances of the old diplomacy. Thus Marshal Foch of France was strangely disinterested in plans for

[1] Harold Nicolson, *Peacemaking, 1919* (Constable, 1934).

the disarmament of Germany; he just did not believe that Germany would stay disarmed. What he sought was the Rhine as France's frontier, across which he did not think the enemy would so easily pass. But this conflicted with Wilson's principle of the self-determination of peoples, for the left bank of the Rhine has a large German population. The peace treaty instead provided that the British Commonwealth and the U.S.A. were to give France a guarantee of their automatic assistance if Germany attacked again–a powerful deterrent, since Germany might well consider the whole Anglo-Saxon world in combination ultimately invincible. Moreover, the Rhineland was to be occupied by the Allies for a period and a strip extending fifty kilometres east of the Rhine was to remain permanently unfortified, leaving, as it were, an open door to the French armies. Yet the Covenant of the League of Nations in its final form did not provide for armed intervention against an aggressor, but only for economic sanctions (i.e. an embargo on trade).

The treaty of peace with Germany was signed at Versailles on Saturday, 28th June 1919. The broad avenue to the palace of Louis XIV, 'le Roi Soleil', was lined with cavalry in steel-blue helmets, the grand staircase flanked by Gardes Republicaines with drawn swords. Clemenceau presided in the two-hundred-year-old Hall of Mirrors, to which the German representatives were brought for the ceremony of signature from the quarters in which they had been penned. In this same hall, in 1871, Bismarck–against a background of Prussian thigh-boots, white breeches, blue tunics and spiked helmets–had declared William I of Prussia to be German Emperor. Now the guns fired as the treaty was signed to announce to Paris and to all of France that the defeat of 1870 had been formally avenged. (The fact that Hitler was also to lord it in that hall was mercifully veiled in the inscrutable future.)

The tragedy of the Treaty of Versailles (and of the subsequent treaties with the other defeated enemies) was twofold: it lay in the loss of moral authority and of American support. The treaties were in fact punitive and were imposed by force. Yet they purported hypocritically to represent principles of abstract justice–and were originally to have been freely negotiated. To the Germans they were therefore from the start something imposed by force and deceit, to be thrown off as quickly as possible by the same means. But the major tragedy occurred when the American Senate refused to ratify the treaty. It had been framed by President Wilson so as to render American co-operation essential. Yet the United States would not honour the American guarantees which President Wilson wished Europe to accept in place of the old diplomacy. France was thus left with neither the Rhine frontier nor the Anglo-American guarantee for which she had so reluctantly relinquished it (for the British guarantee did not operate without the American). A French journalist had remarked earlier in the negotiations that Mr. Wilson's responsibility—if he failed—would be greater than a single human being could bear and survive. Mr. Wilson suffered a paralytic stroke and did not long survive. The U.S.A. did not become a member of the League of Nations; did not (as she has so actively since 1945) co-operate in the solution of post-war problems and remained isolated from the Old World for twenty years.

5

Aftermath, a Comparison

1918, 1945

'I COMMEND the German Reich to your loving care.' Thus—the Kaiser having abdicated–the last Imperial Chancellor addressed the first Chancellor of republican Germany. And Ebert accepted the responsibility entrusted to him with the words: 'For that Reich I have lost two sons.' The Germans gained representative government in place of government by an hereditary emperor, and–unlike the Russians–they went no further. Ebert inaugurated a period of constitutional government; there was nothing comparable to the Communist dictatorship, and those few revolutionaries who tried to follow the Russian pattern were sternly suppressed in bitter street-fighting. The German Army retreated with unbroken discipline from the countries it had invaded to its undamaged homeland, to find, however, a real shortage of food in the cities, for the blockade of Germany continued until mid-January 1919. It was not until the summer that considerable imports of food actually began to reach Germany. Moreover, the Germans were faced with the Allies' demand for astronomical reparations. True, these reparations were in the event never fully paid and what was paid was more than offset by loans from American financiers. Reparations were, however, of great significance in two ways. They convinced the Germans more than ever of the injustice of the peace treaty enforced upon them. Their non-payment also led the French in 1922 to occupy the Ruhr, the heart of industrial Germany.

The German reply to this was a general strike of all workers in the Ruhr, to whom the Government undertook to pay relief.

The finances of the new German state were already strained and this new burden proved too much. The Government printed more and more mark notes, but the goods to be bought with these notes by no means increased in like proportion, so that the currency started to lose its value. Thus began the greatest inflation the world had ever seen, for the Germans lost faith in their own currency and the wheel began to spin faster and faster, until the men who had first set it moving were powerless to stop it. The worker hurried to spend his pay the day it was received, for if he waited even until the following morning it would buy less. Not only price labels in the shops but even postage stamps were overprinted with new values.[1] Additional strings of noughts were added to the actual currency notes as the printing presses strove to keep abreast of the process which the printing presses had started. The savings of a lifetime sufficed suddenly for no more than a single meal; what had been a handsome legacy, an acceptable dowry became valueless. Rents were still controlled by war-time legislation, and eventually a month's rent—say, 150 marks—was less than the cost of an evening paper, when a single issue was valued in thousands of marks. A tram ticket might cost 2,000,000,000,000 marks, for eventually £1 was worth 43,000,000,000,000. At that stage the currency was repudiated and a new one introduced, limited in quantity so that its value was guaranteed by the goods it represented. But the savings of the middle class had been wiped out and its members found themselves without that security, that cushion against the jolts of ill-luck, accident and illness which had helped to differentiate them from the manual workers. It was upon their fears and resentment that Hitler was later to play so successfully. And the horror of unbridled inflation remains at the back of the German mind, a potential source of panic.

At home, fear of unemployment led to a scheme to release 'key men' first. These key men—those whose skill was expected to make employment available for others—were not unnaturally very often those who had come into the Army last and had seen least, if any, of the trench warfare. This was too much even for

[1] Many shops left the price labels unchanged but displayed an easily changeable card indicating the factor by which the prices were to be multiplied.

4. Mr. Asquith (right) in 1912
(Picture Post Library)

Mr. Lloyd George and Mr. Winston Churchill in 1915
(Topical Press)

Picture Post

5. The Suffragette

6. Food Queue, 1917

Associated New

the discipline which had withstood the strain of Passchendaele and of the French mutinies in 1917. There was intense resentment and impatience; mutinies in the camps at Folkestone and Dover; Epsom Police Station was stormed and there was even some loss of life at Kinmel Park. Mr. Churchill became War Minister in the middle of January 1919 and his first act was to institute release according to length of service and age, with immediate discharge for those wounded on three or more occasions. Nevertheless, before this change could be understood throughout the Army, there was a mutiny in Calais, where a number of supply and line-of-communication units had to be surrounded and disarmed by two divisions of front-line troops.

Sir Winston Churchill recounts a dramatic episode—his life is throughout the stuff of drama—which gives an impression of the feeling of the time, so different from our own, and which took place in the heart of London. At breakfast time on 8th February 1919 he was urgently summoned to the War Office because some 3,000 soldiers due to return to France from leave had refused to entrain and instead marched from Victoria to Whitehall, where they now formed a mob in the Horse Guards Parade, disorderly and armed. After consultations Mr. Churchill requested the Chief of the Imperial General Staff and the General Officer Commanding London District to surround and make prisoners of the mutinous 3,000. 'I remained in my room a prey to anxiety,' he writes. 'Ten minutes passed slowly. From my windows I could see the Life Guards on duty in Whitehall closing the gates and doors of the archway.'[1] He could see a number of civilians watching from the roof of the Horse Guards the remarkable scene which was obscured from his own view, namely that of the Grenadier Guards advancing slowly with fixed bayonets from the one side, while the Household Cavalry advanced similarly on the armed mob from the other. To his intense relief common sense and discipline prevailed. The 3,000 allowed themselves to be shepherded to Wellington Barracks—where they were given a good breakfast before resuming the journey to France.

The year 1919 saw a welter of strikes: it was as if the storm which was interrupted by the greater savagery of war had

[1] *The World Crisis, the Aftermath.*

E

suddenly burst with the removal of the international distraction. The strikes in 1919 surpassed all previous records. In 1912 (easily the worst pre-war year) 40,890,000 working days were lost, in 1921 85,872,000. By contrast, since 1934 the highest figure has been 3,687,000 in 1944, with lower figures in the years that followed.[1] Socialism seemed then to have been established in Russia and this powerfully influenced the aspirations of the British Labour Party and trade unions, although revolutionary socialism of the Continental type had few adherents in Britain, apart from the Clyde and the Rhondda Valley.

After the short-lived boom of 1918–20 there was unemployment and much suffering, as men who had survived the war now found themselves struggling bitterly to get a foothold in civilian life, to achieve security enough to support a wife and enjoy bringing up children. The financial climate was radically different from that of our day, for in 1925 the value of the pound sterling was again linked to that of the 'international currency' gold. This meant that British goods previously priced at, say, 18s. now automatically cost the foreigner 20s., which naturally hampered exports, and that at a time of growing unemployment. As export prices had to be reduced so had costs–and consequently wages, at a time when there was at best an uneasy truce after the welter of strikes.

Coal was perhaps the industry which suffered most. It had always been badly organised and was now facing renewed German competition. The coal-owners of that day, and their fathers before them, had been niggardly in investing in the mines the modern equipment and layouts they needed, while a legacy of bitterness between miner and owner had been passed down the generations, and had in no way been dispelled by the war. The coal-owners, forced to lower prices, decided to reduce wages, which would have made mining one of the worst-paid employments, as it was already the most dangerous. A Royal Commission was set up under Lord Samuel (it was not the first) and reported in March 1926 in favour of re-equipment and reorganisation, with a temporary reduction in wages. Neither party accepted the recommendation and the mines ceased to wind coal on 30th April.

---

[1] Figures from G. D. H. Cole, *Introduction to Trade Unionism* (Allen & Unwin, 1953).

The secretary of the Miners' Federation, A. J. Cook, raised the famous battle-cry, 'Not a penny off the pay, not a minute on the day' and the newly-formed Trades Union Congress voted to support the miners by a national strike of all unions beginning at midnight on 3rd May.

'When the bells rang at midnight on Monday over the silent cities, they announced the beginning of a stillness which nobody had ever known before in English history. The Council (of the T.U.C.) had said that all activities should cease, in the trades that it named, and cease they did. There were no trains, no bus services, no trams, no papers, no building, no power.'[1] The first and only 'general' strike in British history took place in 1926– 'postponed' from 1914. Its immediate causes are still a matter of controversy: one of the strongest characters on the unions' side, Mr. Ernest Bevin, is but recently dead; Mr. Winston Churchill (who called Mr. Bevin to be Minister of Labour in 1940) emerged at once as one of the most active members on the Government side. The survivors are still with us of a generation whose bitterness has not been effaced by a second world war, but the probability is that the last-minute negotiations between Government and T.U.C. collapsed because the extremists on either side welcomed the opportunity for the long-postponed trial of strength. Yet there is evidence that the General Council of the T.U.C. was anxious to avoid drastic action, although it is doubtful whether they could have controlled the miners.

The strike lasted nine days. Hyde Park was used as a milk depot; troops were stationed in Whitehall; the T.U.C. kept itself informed by a service of despatch riders. It allowed some lorries to move if brightly placarded in black on yellow: 'Permit from the T.U.C.' Firms made arrangements for their office staffs to live in hotels, but some walked fifteen to twenty miles a day to and from work, while private cars were crammed and enthusiastic middle-class amateurs drove occasional buses and trains. The T.U.C. called it off on 13th May. The dockers, printers and transport workers remained on strike another five days, the miners another six months until once again they were starved

[1] G. D. H. Cole and Raymond Postgate, *The Common People, 1746–1946* (Methuen, 4th ed., 1949).

back to work—and during the next few years a quarter of a million people left South Wales. It is all part of the background to the nationalisation of the coal-mines after the Second World War.

Strangely this contrasts with the pictures of 1945, for those who survived to fight the Second World War had not forgotten the lessons of the First. In the summer of 1945 the German armies were obliged to fight until they were totally overwhelmed, and their enemies from east and west met in the middle of the Reich. This time there was no question of laying down their arms and returning to their undamaged homes. Shell-fire, street-fighting and the passage of hostile armies followed on tremendous aerial bombardment. The Germans themselves blew up every bridge as they retreated, but behind them nearly 40 per cent of their homes had already been destroyed by high-explosive and fire bombs.[1] We know now that the damage to industry was a good deal less than we expected, that bulging walls, a corrugated-iron roof and gaping windows in a sea of rubble often concealed machinery that still worked, and that even machinery buried under tons of fallen masonry could be rescued and restored surprisingly quickly by men whose livelihood depended on it. Yet a city of which acres at a stretch have been reduced to waist-high rubble—with its damp, bitter smell, its fine, penetrating dust and sometimes wreaths laid by survivors where there are still bodies in the rubble—presents pictures which remain in the minds of those who saw them and may have a lasting effect on the generation which lived surrounded by this massive destruction of familiar things. In the end broken-down tramcars and tanks were left across the pavement, willowherb and tall grass covered the square outside the silent railway station. A family could be seen emerging, incongruously neat, from the basement stairway into the gutted shell of their house.[2] In this destruction 'displaced persons' were suddenly free to wander—slaves who had been brought in to work for the German war machine, groups uprooted from the

[1] If these percentages can be trusted, this indicates an overall destruction of dwellings just about ten times as great as that suffered in the United Kingdom.
[2] It is interesting to contrast Sir Harold Nicolson's pained description of Vienna in 1919: 'The town has an unkempt appearance: paper lying about: the grass plots round the statues are strewn with litter: many windows broken and repaired by boards nailed up.'

countries the Germans had overrun. Into this destruction Western Germany was also later to receive and accommodate 8 millions of her own refugees from the zone occupied by the Russians and from lost provinces in the east.

For this time there was no strictly constitutional revolution, no passing of responsibility from one Chancellor to another. Government broke down. It was replaced by the stern military government of the victorious Allied armies, which became less stern and increasingly paternal as time went on. For it was the task of military government to restore German social life: first food, water, sanitation, public security and communications, then local government and ultimately central government, for this time the Western Allies regarded the rehabilitation of shattered Germany as their liability. Before the end of the fighting the United Nations Relief and Rehabilitation Administration had been set up to amass supplies of all those goods of which the enemy-dominated territories of the world must be assumed to be in need. As each port became available Unrra's uniformed officials poured in stocks of food, fuel and medicine, of fertilisers, vehicles and farm machinery for the relief of civilian populations, the United Nations 'being determined that immediately upon the liberation of any area . . . the population thereof shall receive aid and relief from their sufferings, food, clothing and shelter, aid in the prevention of pestilence and in the recovery of the health of the people. . . .' Before it was wound up Unrra had distributed some £1,000 million of aid in a generally successful effort to give more body to the thin blood of the populations from whom we had been cut off and to set it circulating more vigorously again. It was an imaginative undertaking to set in the balances against the ghastly inhumanities of the war. Although for about two years rations in Germany were dangerously low, there were no epidemics, such as the influenza which added so greatly to the loss of life after the First War. In all, the Germans received some $4,000 million worth of Western aid and paid only about one-eighth of that sum in reparations to the Western Allies.[1]

[1] These and the subsequent figures in this chapter are given in dollars owing to the change in the external value of sterling in 1949. As a rule of thumb, dollar totals may be divided by four to give sterling equivalents before 1949 and by three thereafter.

This time the United States, now incomparably the richest and most powerful nation of the world, did not turn away and isolate herself from Europe, but accepted the leadership which events thrust upon her. America at that time was supporting Europe, and American officials influencing policy in every European capital. In 1946 the French received $1,250 million and Britain a loan of $3,750 million. On 5th June 1947 General Marshall, then United States Secretary of State, announced the plan which will go into history under his name. It was designed to prime the pump of European production, and its purpose was achieved. The United Kingdom and the nations of the European continent were to work out together how far they could meet each other's needs and were then to submit their joint requests to the United States for the aid they were unable to give each other. The U.S.S.R. and the Communist governments of eastern Europe took no part, but in April 1948 seventeen countries (plus the Free State of Trieste) formed the Organisation for European Economic Co-operation. O.E.E.C. is one of the several sets of cryptic initials which mark the uncertain striving of the European nations towards some form of union which will combine their several small sovereignties into one great power—or at least will give them as many of the advantages of union as can be purchased for the amount of sovereignty each is willing to yield. It is worth remarking that President Wilson's emphasis after the First World War was all on the self-determination of peoples: almost regardless of damage to the network of trade and communication he was insistent, at least in theory, that each ethnically distinct population should form its own self-governing state. His successors show impatience with Europe's plenitude of little sovereign states (little by comparison with the nations of North and South America), each with its ancient national pride and jealousies, its different currency, frontiers and trade barriers. The weight of their influence has been decidedly given to the idea of a united Europe.

Between 3rd April 1948 and the end of 1951 the eighteen states of O.E.E.C. received aid under the Marshall Plan to the value of over $12,285,000,000. Since then the United States has given further vast sums, in 1962 £1,800 million, to the under-developed countries, which are striving to industrialise and to raise their peoples from poverty. The Plan was administered by Mr. Averell Harriman, who, as chief of American Lend-Lease during the war, had already 'given away more money than any individual in the previous history of the world' [1]–for Lend-Lease signified that the Allies contributed both treasure and blood to each other's war effort, recognising that money spent on the engines of war yields no commercial return and that the treasure can no more be refunded than the blood.

The Marshall Plan meant that the U.S.A. was spending $10 million every twenty-four hours to sustain Europe. The American journalist Mr. Theodore H. White has most graphically described what this involved: 'In the winter of 1950, when Europe's pulse had revived from a flicker to a beat, and the Plan was in full flood, I checked the movement of ships to one country, France, alone. On that day, the s.s. *Godrun Maersk* . . . came . . . to dock at Rouen and unload Marshall Plan tractors, chemicals, synthetic resin and cellulose acetate. Sixty miles down-river from Rouen, at Le Havre, on the same day, the s.s. *Cape Race* . . . checked in with another load of general cargo. And on that same day, 500 miles to the south, the s.s. *Gibbes Lykes* pulled up the narrow, twisting ships' channel of Marseilles with 3,500 tons of Gulf Coast sulphur. In the next three days ten more American ships weighed in around the rim of France. Into their dirty holds the Marshall Plan had stuffed tyres, borax, aircraft parts and drilling equipment on the s.s. *Samuel Stranger*; farm machines, chemicals, on the s.s. *Rhondda*; 2,500 more tons of sulphur on the s.s. *Shirley Lykes*; and, of course, cotton–on the s.s. *Geirulo*, s.s. *Delmundo*, s.s. *Lapland*, s.s. *Cotton States*, s.s. *Velma Lykes*. . . . By that date, in February of 1950, over one thousand ships had un-loaded Marshall Plan cargo in France alone. To keep all Europe going, at any given moment of the day or night, there were an estimated 150 ships either bringing Marshall Plan cargo to Europe on the high seas or unloading it in her ports.' [2]

The Marshall Plan paid for the draining of malarial swamps in Sardinia, new dykes against the Zuyder Zee, the mechanisation

---

[1] Theodore H. White, *Fire in the Ashes, Europe in Mid-century* (Cassell, 1954). Mr. Churchill called America's supply of goods under Lend-Lease 'The most unselfish and unsordid financial act of any country in all history'.
[2] Theodore H. White, *op. cit.*

of the French coal-mines, the building of hydro-electric power stations. With its help European production was overall 45 per cent higher in 1950 than it had been in 1947 and was even 25 per cent above the level of 1938. By contrast, after the First War the United States insisted on the repayment of war debts (although the residue was ultimately repudiated by the European debtors) and President Calvin Coolidge tersely expressed that earlier American point of view when he remarked: 'They hired the money, didn't they?'

Equally striking is the contrast at home between post-war 1918 and post-war 1945. The end of the Second World War saw the formation for the first time of a Labour Government with a large majority over both Conservatives and Liberals combined, independent at last of Liberal support and able to push through Parliament a great deal of the programme which the Labour Party had thrashed out in the thirty-five years since its formation. This Government the trade unions had no desire to embarrass. On the contrary, they co-operated loyally in the wage restraint called for by that 'austere dedicated figure' Sir Stafford Cripps. Such strikes as took place during the first half-dozen years following the Second War were nearly all 'unofficial' and against the wishes of the trade-union leaders. Nor was there much to strike about in those years. On the political side the Welfare State was taking shape in a series of major Acts of Parliament. On the industrial side there were jobs for all, and to spare, at rising wages. The pent-up demand for goods, which naturally awaits the switch-over of factories from munitions to civilian production, and the resumption of house-building were fortified after 1945 by a continuing but not uncontrolled inflation, due to the fact that rising wages and the social services were handing out money more rapidly than the corresponding goods could be made available.

This steady pressure of inflation kept industrial activity and employment at a high level, even when the first flush of post-war orders had been executed. After 1950 the active rearmament which followed on the outbreak of fighting in Korea brought in fresh orders. But the inflationary flow which carried high employment at home had its disadvantages in trade with other countries —on which Britain depends. The high tide at home was somewhat like water raised up by the lock gates in a canal: when in 1947 we attempted to make sterling freely convertible into other currencies Britain's gold and dollar reserves rushed out like the water when the lock gates are opened, and the experiment had forthwith to be discontinued. (The fact that this was due to a variety of factors, of which our inflation was only a minor one, we reserve for examination later on.) In 1949 there was another crisis in our external trade and it became impossible to hold the level of the water on our side: we had to 'devalue' sterling so that £1 became worth only $2·80 instead of $4·03. Two years later there was another crisis. Moreover, the lock gates which dammed up the water took the form of rigid financial and trade controls, the rationing of food, coal and clothes, of steel and raw materials. Englishmen became the most penurious of travellers abroad, while they were totally unable to visit the U.S.A. except for reasons of business approved by the Treasury. Food rationing had only been generally introduced towards the end of the First World War, in March 1918, and food coupons were abolished in May of the next year, followed quickly by the removal of bread rationing in August. The last restriction, that on sugar, had vanished by November 1920. By contrast bread rationing was not actually introduced in the Second World War until after the Germans had collapsed, when it was applied in this country in order to make more wheat available for them. Food rationing continued in diminishing degree for nine long years after the end of the war, but this was partly due to the use of fixed rations at controlled prices as a means of securing 'fair shares for all'.

6

The Great Depression

1929–1938

THE world slump of 1929–33 was the most dramatic event which took place between the wars, for the second of which it is partly responsible (for it is arguable that but for the massive unemployment and suffering in Germany the Nazi madness would never have spread as it did). The depression has also left its lasting mark on the British working man who experienced it–an impression which even the Second War and the changed outlook of to-day seem powerless to remove. It is a memory that will probably only die with the generations which experienced those years of unwilling idleness, or which left school to hang about unwanted at the street corner.

In its external manifestations the great slump was nothing if not spectacular. We read of the burning of wheat crops, the payment of subsidies to American farmers to reduce the acreage sown, of coffee dumped by the shipload in the Atlantic or used to heat furnaces, of insect pests introduced into the plantations to check the surfeit of rubber. In the world markets even in 1938 the price of cotton was still only one-third that of 1924, that of wool one-half. Between 1929 and 1932 the value of world trade in raw materials fell by more than a half, by nearly one-half in foodstuffs and by more than one-third in manufactures. At the worst moment, in 1932, there were in the world 30 million people anxious to work and unable to find jobs. The unemployed in Britain totalled nearly 3 million.

The onset and political repercussions of the economic crisis were equally dramatic. In the United States speculation in stocks and shares had become a national craze–almost comparable to betting on the Pools in this country. Families with no pretensions to being financiers–and with none of the financier's background knowledge–bought and sold shares on the Stock Exchange; and made money as share quotations went booming upward. A situation was created in which shares were bought and sold at prices which a sober calculation of their possible earnings could never justify. Vast numbers of expensive goods had also been sold on hire purchase. The inescapable reckoning came on 24th October 1929, when the bottom began to fall out of the New York Stock Exchange. Prices fell almost overnight and savings disappeared; those who had speculated wildly paid a bitter penalty. But the interrelations of the financial world are delicate and the repercussions of the American financial crisis spread rapidly outwards. Great sums had been loaned to Germany and often invested in plant, machinery or municipal building. When the Americans, short of cash, ceased foreign lending and began to call for repayment of their loans the strain became too much for the Germans. The first crack was the failure in 1931 of the great Austrian bank, the Kreditanstalt, followed rapidly by the report that one of the biggest German banks was also in difficulties. Those were the days when heads of State banks hastened frantically from capital to capital, trying to shore up the crumbling walls. The Bank of England granted Germany a loan of £70 million and President Hoover then secured general consent to a moratorium on German debt payments.

In Britain meanwhile the unemployment insurance fund was bankrupt and the long-term unemployed became a direct burden on the Exchequer. The May Committee reported in July 1931 that the Exchequer was running into debt at the rate of more than £100 million a year, and this calculation was not only a shock to public opinion in Britain but had the more unfortunate effect of upsetting confidence abroad, so that the foreign money which is normally deposited in London began to flow rapidly homewards, thus adding to the drain on British reserves. 'In the early autumn of 1931,' wrote Mr. Somervell four years later, 'citizens in every walk of life were preparing themselves for a winter of such distressful emergencies as had not been experienced in living memory. Many expected that the pound would go the way of the mark and the rouble, that the comfortable would lose their savings and the uncomfortable would starve.'[1] The Labour Government was dependent on Liberal support, inexperienced and not united. Mr. Ramsay MacDonald, the Prime Minister, resolved his crisis by resigning on behalf of himself and his Cabinet, but at the request of the King returned to office at the head of a new Cabinet, ostensibly 'National'–that is, a combination of all parties united to ride out the storm–but actually pretty well dependent on Conservative support. The bitterness which at that time surrounded MacDonald–to the Labour rank and file a renegade–lingers still to-day (but it is interesting that nearly twenty years earlier Beatrice Webb had already written in her diary, 'J. R. MacDonald has ceased to be a Socialist').

Mr. Snowden introduced a second Budget in the autumn and an Economy Act was passed which reduced the salaries of all civil servants–Ministers, judges, teachers, the armed forces, postmen, police–and the relief payments to the unemployed. In September 1931 Britain again abandoned the gold standard and the value of the pound sterling was allowed to fall in terms of gold. Within a year forty nations had followed her example, so that the relative trading position of these countries remained substantially unchanged, although France and Switzerland did not devalue their currencies until 1936.

The economic crisis also brought about a more fundamental change, the abandonment of the principle of Free Trade, which had stood for nearly a century. This was the policy which had made Britain the biggest' customer for the rest of the world, which had led to her importing at one time well over one-third of the goods consumed by her population. Her great industries had not needed the device of tariffs and import duties to protect them–a device that works by the Government placing a tax on imported goods so as to raise their price to British consumers, thus giving an advantage to home-produced goods. But in 1931 for the first time British exports and services rendered to foreigners (plus interest from overseas loans) failed to pay fully for the year's imports and we started to live on capital. In 1932 the

[1] Donald Somervell, *The Reign of King George the Fifth* (Faber, 1935).

principle of Free Trade was abandoned and the policy of Protection, for which Joseph Chamberlain had campaigned so fer-
vently in 1903 and for which he had unsuccessfully spent himself,
was introduced by his son Neville Chamberlain. The Import
Duties Act of that year placed a duty of 10 per cent on all imported goods except those from the Dominions, and this was soon
raised on a number of articles, notably on steel products, to
20 per cent or 33⅓ per cent. In Joseph Chamberlain's lifetime his
cousin had most succinctly defined the difficulty of imposing
tariffs when he said: 'I don't think they will vote for Protection
because I can't think they will be so silly as to ask the Government
to tax the food they eat, the clothes they wear and all the commodities they use, on the promise of politicians that their wages
will rise.' The main difficulty was now removed by the fall in the
cost of food owing to the world-wide depression and slump in
agricultural prices. Home agriculture was now protected by imposing duties on all imports (except meat and wool), which
simply prevented prices falling as much as they would otherwise
have done. In the 'thirties British industry in general was defeatist,
afraid of competition, tending to seek protected areas in which
to make a cosy profit without much effort, to maintain prices
by restricting output. The declining industries of the nineteenth
century sought protection against inevitable economic change.

Whereas at home there was this tendency to settle down to a
dour siege economy, across the Atlantic the new American President Franklin D. Roosevelt was counter-attacking his country's
economic troubles in the liveliest way and with a number of not
wholly consistent expedients. Himself physically handicapped,
he was one of the most forceful and greatest men of our time,
and the one who sat at the seat of unquestionably the greatest
power. Nor had he the opportunity of quiescence, for when he
took office in the spring of 1933 the small private banks of the
American countryside were failing in dozens. Almost his first
action was necessarily to declare a moratorium, to prevent a
panic as the people vainly besieged the bank counters to withdraw
their savings. Fundamentally Roosevelt and his advisers considered
the American depression a crisis of confidence and they set out
to stimulate the U.S.A. to heave itself out of the trough by its

own bootstraps–an exercise at which the Americans are superior
to us. Failure of the normal demand for commodities and services
seemed to be a main cause of the trouble, and the Administration
determined to spend public funds freely so as to put money into
people's pockets and to stimulate private spending. This, of
course, was the reverse of the British Government's decision to
reduce public spending and to cut the salaries of its servants.
Unfortunately two contradictory theories underlay Roosevelt's
actions. One was to raise prices and thus stimulate profits so as to
bring about a business recovery. The other was to raise wages
more than prices and thus stimulate demand. But this–since wages
are costs–reduced profits. The two policies neutralised each
other.

The scale of the conceptions underlying the Roosevelt New
Deal, the vastness and vigour of the experiment are too great for
us to follow. Here was a country of immense real wealth, but
with 14 million unemployed (and at that time no form of unemployment insurance to stand between the workless and starvation or the 'bread line', i.e. the queue for food provided by
private charity). President Roosevelt initiated a social-security
New Deal. There was also a relief New Deal for the unemployed,
for debtors and for farmers. There was a New Deal for labour,
with regulation of working conditions; for the control of speculation; for 'trust-busting'; for progressive taxation: in sum this
aspect of the Administration's activity amounted to what we
should term a mildly socialist programme. It was the great recovery New Deal which was intended to prime the pump of
private spending by public spending. The National Industrial
Recovery Act of June 1933 authorised the President to spend
$3,300 million on public works and to establish a code of
business practices in each industry designed to ensure 'fair competition'–that is, enough competition for efficiency but not so
much as to make business unprofitable. Six hundred codes were
approved covering over 2 million firms–business correspondence
began to come into this country embellished with the U.S. eagle
poised in one corner over the letters N.R.A. (National Recovery
Administration) and the number of the code to which the firm's
practices were to conform.

June 1933 also saw the assembling of the World Economic Conference in London. 'These were the days of conference after conference–wheat conferences, tariff truce conferences, reparations and debt conferences, disarmament conferences–exchanges of diplomatic visits and the desperate endeavour of governments to raise money–real money–in a world overflowing with riches, days in which the grotesque bulks nearly as largely as the tragic.'[1] The United States had left the gold standard in April and it was confidently expected that the new exchange value of the dollar would be revealed to the assembled delegates. No country was willing to commit itself to a trade policy without knowing the answer to this question, for already then, as Sir Dennis Robertson has put it in a survey of recent times, the throbs of America's giant heart rocked the world's boat. On 3rd July President Roosevelt announced that for the time being he was unwilling to recommend any stable value for the dollar; thereafter the conference languished and broke up. This was the last effort to cope with the economic crisis by international agreement. Thereafter world trade was left to look after itself, while each country struggled to mitigate the effects of the depression on its own citizens, for modern governments depending on popular support cannot stand aside when their citizens are idle and hungry. 'In the 'twenties,' reports Professor Lewis, 'economists write of current events as meteorologists write of sun and rain. Whether conditions will improve or deteriorate is taken as a matter beyond human control. . . . In the 'thirties . . . this attitude disappears altogether; it comes to be regarded as the duty of governments to alter and control the course of economic events. . . . The war has still further heightened the contrast; the belief (is now) that governments can entirely determine the course of economic events.'[2]

[1] R. T. Clark, *The Fall of the German Republic* (Allen & Unwin, 1935). Mr. Malcolm Muggeridge also has a pretty picture of these conferences in 'many little towns by lakes, by the sea, suddenly crowded, their quiet disturbed by the tapping of typewriters, buzzing conversation; flags flying over their Hotel Bristol, Hotel Beau Rivage, detectives lounging where ordinarily were picture-postcard sellers'–*The Thirties: 1930–40 in Great Britain* (Hamilton, 1940).

[2] W. Arthur Lewis, *Economic Survey, 1919–1939* (Allen & Unwin, 1949). It was the feats of organisation achieved by governments in the First World War which heightened the ordinary citizen's expectations of what they could do in peace.

Seen down the perspective of the years, the Great Depression was part of the cycle of booms and slumps which is probably unavoidable if we are to retain freedom of choice in our personal consumption and not to have it centrally planned. But so severe a depression need never recur, for an ordinary industrial depression coincided with a severe financial crisis—centred in the U.S.A. and spreading outwards—and with a crisis in agriculture, the whole aggravated by post-war maladjustments and the payment of reparations and war debts. It is equivalent to saying that while thunderstorms, even severe ones, are inevitable (until we learn to control the weather), no one of us need ever experience another hurricane. American controls on speculation and banking are now much stronger; the possibilities and the effects of Government interference in the trade cycle are better understood, and we have become clear in our minds that 'every man for himself' is a recipe for drowning. International organisations of some experience now exist.

The main cause of the Great Depression was unquestionably the slump in agriculture. Between 1913 and 1928, owing to mechanisation, world output of raw materials rose by 40 per cent, that of food by 16 per cent, but world population by only 10 per cent. There was an over-abundance of cheap food and raw materials. Prices fell drastically, cutting the income of great groups of people; the American and Canadian farmers, rubber-growers in Malaya, the producers of rice, wheat, meat and dairy products in S.E. Asia, S. America, Australia and New Zealand all found themselves unable to buy the manufactured products with which the industrial nations normally supplied them. And the slump thus spread to the industrialised areas: Britain, Pittsburg and the eastern states of the U.S.A., Belgium and the Ruhr. The depression was most severe in the U.S.A. and—partly owing to the sudden cessation of American lending—in Germany. In Britain there was less of an acute crisis, but then the position of Great Britain had been unhappy ever since the end of the post-war boom. In 1925, when world trade again exceeded its pre-war level, British exports were actually lower than in 1913: we had already seen other countries creeping up on us, but this was the first time we actually started to move downhill. Between the wars

Britain remained too faithful to her old staple industries, especially textiles. The Japanese were producing cotton piece-goods more cheaply, and in any case many countries now made such goods for themselves. The number of unemployed was never below a million throughout the whole period in Britain; it averaged 14·2 per cent of insured workers as against the 4·8 per cent of the years 1883–1913. But what is most noticeable is that the coal-mining villages, the cotton towns of Lancashire and those dependent on their shipyards–Yarrow, the Clyde–had double this proportion of unemployed. During these years of painful adjustment the numbers of coal-miners and of cotton workers fell by one-third; we built only one-third of the world's new merchant ships instead of three-fifths. Whole towns became silent and oppressed, while there was a steady movement of population from the old centres of Britain's greatness to the newer light industries of the south.

May we at this point glance both backwards and forwards for the sake of the long view? If we look at Britain in 1820 we see no longer an 'undeveloped economy', offering on the world markets only the products of agriculture or mining. There were already manufacturers and only about a third of the occupied population was employed in agriculture and fishing, but there was a 'normal' balance in our affairs: we imported only about one-seventh of what we ate, and this was largely made up of things which will not grow here. Even in 1870 we still produced three-quarters of our own food.

During the course of the nineteenth century Britain gained a world ascendancy such as no nation had ever had before, or is likely to enjoy again–an ascendancy which she could not reasonably hope to maintain. British capital helped to build the vast railways of the North American continent, British shipyards launched the world's merchant ships, British engineers installed the gas-works of Rio Grande do Sul, the Norwegian railways, the trams of Cologne. This supremacy was based on a unique concentration of scientific knowledge, capital and practical 'know-how'. The spread of this knowledge was in those days slow–other nations lacked the background and the skilled mechanics. The United States was then in a position roughly comparable, from

F

the point of view of world trade, to that of Africa to-day; Germany, Japan and Belgium were not industrialised. When other countries also began to develop their own industries and become less dependent on us, Britain added to her earnings by carrying on an abnormal share of the world's shipping, insurance and other commercial services. Sterling was the currency of world trade and the bill of exchange on London its instrument. Consequently in Britain in 1911 there were a great many more men occupied in commerce and finance than in farming.

During the nineteenth century Britain thus became rather like some sea sponge, gaining its livelihood on the flow of world trade, importing enormous quantities of goods and paying for them by massive exports, just as a sponge might get its nourishment by passing quantities of sea-water through its body. By 1911 less than one man in ten was occupied in agriculture and well over half our food was imported. In 1913 we imported seven-eighths of our raw materials, other than coal. We paid for them by exports—that is, largely with the goods we manufactured out of these raw materials from other countries; with the cloth we made for India out of American cotton and the machinery made from Swedish iron ore.

Between the wars the cost of imported food and raw materials was much lower, owing to the slump. In relation to the prices we got for our exports, imports cost 30 per cent less in 1938 than in 1913. Except for those who were out of work, the standard of living for this reason actually rose steadily and quite steeply in the maligned nineteen-twenties and nineteen-thirties. Also one-fifth of our imports were then paid for out of the income from our foreign investments. Came the Second World War and we were obliged to sell £1 billion of overseas investments and found ourselves, at its end, with debts to the tune of £3 billion. Our net income from overseas investments was halved; but worse than this—the Second War left a shortage of food and raw materials throughout the world. As a result we had to pay for our imports at a price which (in relation to what we got for our exports) was in 1947 15 per cent higher than in the ten years before the war and which rose temporarily in 1951 to be over 40 per cent higher.

Imports were cut down to an austerity level, but to pay for them we found ourselves by 1948 exporting at least 50 per cent more in volume than in 1938 and by 1951 80 per cent more, which is no mean achievement.[1] The trade in exports has shifted farther from the old nineteenth-century staples of cotton, woollens and coal and now we depend largely on exports of the most complicated machinery like vehicles, jet aircraft, calculating machines and other electronic devices. These things can still only be made by countries with generations of accumulated skill and with great specialised installations, such as motor-car factories are to-day. As a result we find that whereas in 1931 we had 11,000 mechanical engineers, in 1951 there were 41,000; in 1931 25,000 scientific workers (2·7 per cent women), but in 1951 89,000, of whom 22·2 per cent were women! Yet in this field we can never hope for the same preponderance as we enjoyed last century. Moreover, conditions have moved, probably permanently, in favour of the producers of food and raw materials all over the world—and the Australians and Argentinians are eating more of their own food and selling less, while the countries of the Far East are expecting and needing more.

Never again, almost certainly, will our imports come in as cheaply as between the wars. We shall have to become a little more like we were in 1820. In 1953 our own farms and market gardens produced a good 50 per cent more than in 1938 and in 1965 about half our home food supply came from home production. This proportion may increase.

We have examined the Depression from all aspects except that of the people whose lives were stained by it. In Government circles there was bustle and activity: political crises, enquiries, expedients, international conferences. In the world of the long-term unemployed there was silence broken only by the

[1] It is doubtful whether any major country has made such great changes in the structure of its economy as those made by Britain in the first eight years after the war. Certainly we have adapted ourselves much better than after the First World War and we export a much higher proportion of what we produce than do the countries of the European Economic Community.

voices of Welsh miners' choirs singing in the London streets for food, or by the tramp of 'hunger marchers' from the north, walking down to London in groups organised by some militant leader in order to draw attention to their plight. But the silence was broken by the B.B.C. when it arranged for eleven unemployed men and women to broadcast in 1934. These contemporary, first-hand accounts were published as a book, from which we quote.[1]

W. O'NEILL: 'The other day the teacher asked my little girl what her dad was, and she said, "My dad never works." I'm afraid this is true, because I haven't–barring an odd week or two –had a regular job for the last four years. . . . I was a metal turner –and that's a job that needs seven years' apprenticeship. . . . When I first fell out of work through the firm shutting down, my first feeling was that I at least wouldn't be out of a job long. I used to think that when another man lost his job there must be something wrong with him. I thought I had qualities which would save me from prolonged unemployment. Unfortunately I was soon disillusioned. It is often luck rather than ability that counts. One sees better men than oneself out of work.

'Seeing there was no chance of getting back to my trade, I took any job that came along, and found out to my cost that when one *did* get an opportunity to get back to one's trade, the fact of this casual employment counted against one. The question they always ask one is, "What was your last job?" and as soon as you tell 'em, "Navvying"–they immediately tell you you would be no use to them.

'One gets fed up sometimes looking for a job. What makes it worse is when there is a job going anything up to twelve are sent off for it. That means eleven of us are disappointed, and when this happens over and over again one gets real fed up. We feel we've got skill in our hands and ought to be wanted, instead of having to keep begging for a job. And every day we know this skill gets less, and when we *do* get a job we may find we aren't quick enough for modern requirements. We may not even know the new machinery, and the longer we're out the more desperate it becomes.'

[1] Ed. Felix Greene, *Time to Spare* (Allen & Unwin, 1935).

E. A. G. PARIS: 'I always thought my position was a "safe" one.
I felt secure enough to marry and set up a home. As the years
went by I naturally felt more and more secure, especially as it was
a big and substantial firm and one that had a reputation for giving
their people continuous employment. Some there had been
employed for as long as forty-five years. It was the type of old-
fashioned firm that really seemed to take an interest in its
workers. . . .

'We nearly always went on holiday once a year. Last year we
went to the country—to Bedfordshire. It was near the end of this
holiday, and in fact a year ago to-day, that I received a short note
from my firm telling me "my services were no longer required".
The firm had been absorbed by a large paint combine, and quite
a lot of us were no longer wanted. This was the biggest blow I'd
ever had. It was a terrible shock, and the world which had looked
bright from one moment to another seemed to have absolutely
crashed. The end of our holiday was pretty dismal. I always think
it was unfair to send me that notice while I was on holiday—a
firm that I had been with for over sixteen years.

'After the first shock, when I began to think of the number
of people whom I knew and who could help me, I felt more
hopeful. But this didn't last long, as day after day went by and
I could find nothing. Not only did I go round seeing people, but
sent any number of letters and answers to advertisements. I think
I must have sent over two hundred and fifty letters, but it's just
been a sheer waste of stamps. It's very few firms that even answer
letters, and most of the replies one *does* receive are merely written
on a duplicating machine.'

MRS. PALLAS: 'If only he had work. Just imagine what it would
be like. On the whole, my husband has worked about one year
out of twelve and a half. His face was lovely when I married him,
but now he's skin and bones. When I married he was robust and
he had a good job. He was earning from eight pounds to ten
pounds a week. He's a left-handed ship's riveter—a craft which
should be earning him a lot of money. There aren't many left-
handed riveters. . . .

'He fell out of work about four months after I was married, so
I've hardly known what a week's wage was. Through all the

struggling I've still not lost my respectability. About three or four years ago I could even manage to win a competition for the best-kept home for cleanliness and thrift. The bedclothes were all mended, but they were clean. The originals you could hardly have known for the patches on. My children wouldn't go to school with a hole in their trousers. They come to me. My eldest boy has trousers on at the moment with six patches on them; I just tell him he'll be all the warmer, especially in the winter. My husband helps me with the darning; I do the patching. I've just put the eighth patch into a shirt of his. I take the sleeves out of one and put them in another—anything to keep going.

'Then when we've finished with the clothes, my husband puts them into making a mat. Everything goes in—vests, stockings, linings.

'Many a time I put a bit of black polish on a white thread to put a patch in, because I haven't had any black thread. And often-times I take the buttons off the dirty shirt and put them on the clean, because I haven't the money to buy more buttons if there are some missing.

'Many a time my husband has had to make cups for the children out of empty condensed milk tins. He solders handles on.

'Our kettle's got about six patches on it. My husband made the patches from cocoa tins. My husband does all that sort of patching, all the cobbling and hair-cutting and spring-cleaning. I've always tried to keep my house looking nice. I feel as if I want to be the same as everybody else. So we try each year to put up fresh paper in one room, or whitewash the ceiling or something to freshen things up. My husband does it.

'When I was first married we had the one room. I had the four children in it, and then I had the chance of three rooms, and, though it was twice the rent, I took the responsibility. I have always felt that environment counts. It's the children we feel for. That's what I fight for; it's not for myself. I couldn't expect to bring four children up decently in one room. But it meant not only twice the rent, but I had to furnish them. So I bought sixteen pounds' worth of furniture, and I paid it off week by week out of the dole money. It took nearly two years. . . .

'My husband never changes his dole money, but although he doesn't keep a halfpenny pocket-money, still we can't manage. And we don't waste nothing. And there's no enjoyment comes out of our money—no pictures, no papers, no sports. Everything's patched and mended in our house.

'We're both of us always occupied in the home. I haven't had a holiday for thirteen years. My husband's never been to a football match. When people talk about the talkies (sound films, as against the early silent film) I don't know what they mean. I've never been, but I've no desire to go—it's all gone. . . .

'Some weeks I can get a quarter of a pound of bacon for threepence or threepence halfpenny. Now that eggs are cheap, I use quite a lot. We very, very rarely get cheese. We all like it, but it is a bit of a luxury. When there are birthdays we have it. I can't manage more than one box of matches a week—that's all we ever use. Many a time we've sat in the dark—it is gas light, and we haven't a penny for the slot maybe, or we haven't a match. Rather than let people know, we sat in the dark.

'I do the washing every other week, because I find I can do a large amount of clothes with the same amount of coal and soap, but it is more tiring. . . .

'I don't know to whatever I'll put the boys. I've no idea whatever. I think they ought to know what's happening in the world, but we can't afford any newspaper. . . .

'What's gone is past, but I wouldn't like to live a minute of my life over again. With all the struggling, you can't manage. All the struggling is just for food. Still, we're happier than some, for in our house we're all in harmony, we all help. The kids wash the dishes, and so on. Everyone does something in our house. The only hope we have got is the hope to come. I've lived for hope, or as my husband would say, for faith, for thirteen years.

'Perhaps, after all, it's worse for the men. The women have their work and their home. I have no hope my husband will ever work again.'

JOHN EVANS: 'There are one or two things that I am really glad about. The first is that I live in the Rhondda. There's real kindliness and comradeship there, and that *just* about makes life worth living. The spirit here in this Valley helps to soften many of the hardships of unemployment, although we can't always help each other much with the material things of life.

'The second thing I am glad about is that I haven't a son. It must be a heartbreaking business to watch your boy grow into manhood and then see him deteriorate because there is no work for him to do. And yet there are scores of young men in the Valley who have never worked since the age of sixteen. You see, at sixteen they become insurable, and employers sack them rather than face the extra expense. So we have young men who have never had a day's work since. They have nothing to hope for but aimless drift. I'm glad no son of mine is in that position.

'As I've said, I've been out of work now for eight years, and I've only managed to get eleven days' work in all that time. I'm forty-seven years old, with no hope of work in the future. Work used to shape the whole of my life, and now I've got to face the fact that this won't be so any more.'

The trough of the Depression was reached in 1932, but it was not until the approaching threat of another war galvanised derelict factories and shipyards back to life that jobs became freely available again. In 1937 there were still 1,600,000 workless, and as late as December 1938 a scene took place, in the middle of London and at the height of the Christmas shopping, which it is worth recalling. As the flow of traffic in Oxford Street was halted by the traffic lights 200 unemployed men suddenly lay down across the road. Head to toe, eight abreast, they spread posters over their bodies with the slogan WORK OR BREAD and lay there chanting in unison: 'We want work or bread. We want extra relief.'[1]

As the account shows, the 'dole' kept these men and their families alive, but it was not sufficient to prevent slow physical deterioration, at any rate in the adults. The long-term unemployed with their wives and children bore the brunt of that period's suffering, but in all their misery they preserved their

---

[1] Robert Graves and A. Hodge, *The Long Weekend, a Social History of Great Britain, 1918–39* (Faber, 1950).

balance and political common sense, even their humour, yielding their remaining personal liberty to neither Fascist nor Communist, preferring to violence methods of agitation like the scene in Oxford Street. The only monument which stands out on the dreary plain of Britain between the wars is that erected by these families' grim courage and endurance.

7

Louder and Nearer:

The Approach of the Second World War

THE first distant beat of drums came across the world in September 1931 when the Japanese Army invaded Manchuria—as it transpired without the prior knowledge or consent of the Japanese Government. By successfully imitating the West, Japan had quickly become a Great Power, but without the raw materials and coal which are the sinews of power. Yet these were available in China, and the Japanese militarists decided that they might yet exploit China in the twentieth century as the Western Powers had tended to exploit her in the nineteenth. China promptly appealed to the League of Nations.

This appeal was embarrassing, for one League member had infringed the territorial integrity of another and this demanded the imposition of 'sanctions'—that is, pressure exerted on the aggressor by the whole community of nations. It was, of course, much the same situation as confronted the United Nations Organisation in 1950 in Korea. But the members of the League were not in 1931 an effective community of nations. A committee of enquiry was set up, consisting of twelve members under the chairmanship of M. Briand, the French Foreign Minister. Mr. Matsuoka, Japan's representative, occasionally addressed the committee in Japanese. The word 'war' was never used; the nearest approach to it was a declaration that 'there was a very considerable military element in the Japanese activities'. Mr. Matsuoka assured the committee that his Government wished scrupulously to observe and maintain the principles of the Covenant of the League.

The committee of twelve was succeeded by a committee of nineteen and that by a committee of nine. In January 1932 the Japanese landed at Shanghai and fighting took place on the doorstep of the international settlement there. In Geneva, seat of the League of Nations and 'capital city of the unstable peace between the two world wars', it was decided to appoint a commission of enquiry under the chairmanship of Lord Lytton. But the Japanese objected to the commission travelling to China by the shortest route, which is by the Trans-Siberian Railway, so it went via America and did not arrive until the spring in Manchuria, meanwhile renamed Manchukuo and governed by a 'puppet' administration under Japanese control. The Lytton Commission's report of some 400 pages appeared in October 1932 and avoided calling for the imposition of sanctions by condemning neither party to the dispute, although it demanded that all armed forces should be withdrawn from Manchuria. The moral status of the League of Nations had declined sharply; collective security–the security which was to have been provided by the overwhelming power of the community of nations acting in concert–had failed to protect China. In 1933 the Japanese withdrew from the League and later invaded Jehol. In 1937 came their full-scale attack on China, but this was not even discussed in Geneva.

The Disarmament Conference sat in Geneva from February 1932 until April 1935. France, in accordance with Briand's ideas on European Union, tabled a proposal for an international army controlled by the League of Nations–an idea which does not ring so strange in our ears. (It was in a way intended as a substitute for the Geneva Protocol of 1924, which had aimed at abolishing war by compulsory arbitration; each nation subscribing to the Protocol was to uphold the arbitrators' decision by force of arms. Only France, ever seeking security against Germany, had ratified the Protocol and it thus remained still-born. For the nations were not yet ready, as they are still not ready, to accept compulsory arbitration and to commit themselves to go to war in order to uphold the decisions of an international court.) Sir John Simon, for Britain, then produced a plan for 'qualitative' disarmament, forbidding certain weapons–as we are to-day trying to forbid weapons of mass destruction whose unimaginable horrors were then unknown. It was proposed that bombing from the air should be abolished, but to this Britain was reluctant to consent, for the bombing, after due warning, of villages on the N.W. Frontier of India was the easiest way of maintaining peace. A proposal to limit tanks to eight tons was likewise rejected by the British, who were trying out a new 16-tonner. The French then suggested 70 tons as the limit; at the time they were experimenting with siege tanks of 60 tons. (In the event only four British tanks of 16 tons were built and the development of the big, fast tank was largely left to the Germans.) The atmosphere of the long-drawn-out Disarmament Conference was caught by Ramsay MacDonald when he said that he felt 'day after day as though I was looking upon a stage with something moving immediately behind the footlights, but as if there was something else there of a different character–an ominous background full of shadows and uncertainties'.

Germany was part of this ominous background. Under Stresemann's policy of fulfilling the Allies' demands and publicly co-operating with them, Germany had returned to the comity of nations. Stresemann's policy appeared very similar to that pursued by the Catholic Chancellor Adenauer after Germany's second defeat. His great triumph was to extract from the Allies the promise that their occupation of the Rhineland would end as early as 1930, but Stresemann literally wore himself out and after his death Germany found no leader able to carry the people with him in his policy, to associate the nation with the Government– for the Germans have no long tradition of self-government. Then came the Great Depression and by the end of 1931 there were over 5 million unemployed. 'And so 1931, a year of bitter anxiety, ended, but in a way that must have made many Germans despair of their country. Other nations had alike been involved in crisis and were now in considerably better heart than they had been; even the new, the raw nations, the uncivilised nations, in desperate plight as they were, had held together. Germany had given only an example of panic, disarray and confusion. On a conservative estimate no less than 40 per cent of the nation was behind two extremist parties (the Nazis and the Communists), which sought to make confusion worse confounded in order, apparently, to establish a gang dictatorship . . . it was a prospect calculated to appal the stoutest-hearted patriot; in Germany by 1932 the capacity for being appalled was almost the only faculty which the stout-hearted still seemed to possess.'[1]

With several private armies within the State–the Nationalist 'Stahlhelm', the Nazi Brownshirts, the Socialist 'Reichsbanner', the Communist 'Rotfront'–Germany was on the brink of civil war. Between the two extremes the middle classes should have been a stabilising factor. But the middle classes were very hard hit by the depression, and when, in 1931, 'the spectre of inflation arose, the memories of the horrors of 1923–24 broke down every restraint, and from that moment the bourgeoisie as a class was lost to the cause of law and order. Blindly clutching at the first saviour who offered, it turned instinctively . . . to a man of its own class'[2]–that is, to Hitler. He promised 'higher salaries, lower rents, cheaper food, higher prices . . . security of property, lower taxes and increased social services, lower interest, easy money, and the abolition of debt–all the ingredients of the earthly economic paradise of the little man in a little house with a little business who saw starvation staring himself and his family in the face'.[3] And Hitler was an able demagogue in an age when broadcasting, microphones and amplifiers, and newspapers of mass circulation enable one man to address vast audiences. The sound of a crowd listening to one of Hitler's speeches, wrote the editor of the American periodical *Foreign Affairs*, was a 'surge of voices, as in a menagerie where all the animals have gone mad, but by some trick can still be made to bay and howl in unison'.

Hitler's following and his private army increased. His funds were provided by the great industrialists, intent, for their part, on using him against the Socialists and the organised military units of the Communists. For two years the Prussian land-owners governed by decree. In 1932 there were as many as five general elections. Intriguing constantly for their own narrow interests,

[1] R. T. Clark, *The Fall of the German Republic* (Allen & Unwin, 1935).
[2] R. T. Clark, *op. cit.*
[3] *Ibid.*

but anxious to preserve the appearance and outward form of a democratic government, they eventually invited Hitler to become German Chancellor, intending to hold this uncouth demagogue a prisoner within a Cabinet whose members would be of their own choosing, and thus to use him for their own continued purposes. It was a miscalculation for which they and the world paid dearly, but it was in this manner that Hitler was admitted to power by the servants' entrance and came at length to sit in the seat of Bismarck.

From that point onwards Hitler had only to apply his favourite technique, that of the cuckoo in the nest—a technique with which Communist governments have since his death made us nauseatingly familiar. To this he added stark terror: beating up on the streets, rough-houses in public places, murder. The basic freedoms; freedom of the Press, of speech, of the ballot, and freedom from arbitrary arrest were swept away. Political murder by the Brownshirts the courts came to regard as manslaughter. 'One man's love can permeate the world, and so can one man's hate. The tears which Christ shed as he looked down on Jerusalem filled innumerable other eyes; the pity he felt for men coming and going, passing in and out of doorways and up and down streets, was reproduced in innumerable other breasts. The resentment and self-pity which possessed Hitler when he felt himself scorned and rejected was similarly reproduced. His hatred, passionately stated, proved infectious. It swelled into a mighty roar of hate, echoing and re-echoing through the world.'[1]

The Army, officered by the landed gentry, was by no means happy that Hitler's Nazi Brownshirt formations should have the freedom of the streets, particularly as Roehm, the Brownshirt Chief of Staff, who had been Hitler's colleague and companion from the earliest days of the movement, was known to be imbued with revolutionary ideas. The decision lay in Hitler's hand, and on 30th June 1934, like some avenging pagan god, he took it. He flew unexpectedly to Munich, landing in the small hours of the morning, and between then and the following morning some 5,000 to 7,000 Nazis, including Roehm, were shot by his orders.

[1] Malcolm Muggeridge, *The Thirties*. This remarkable passage must have been written just about the time that war broke out.

Henceforth the Nazis ceased to dream of a social revolution and those who had joined the Brownshirts, some of them idealistic young men, became the servants of the militarism and imperialism which was ultimately to destroy them. Hitler had thrown in his lot with the Army. Later he was to bring the Army under his control. 'This massacre,' as Mr. Winston Churchill remarked, '. . . showed . . . that conditions in Germany bore no resemblance to those of a civilised state.'

Just under a month later the Austrian Nazis mobilised and about lunchtime an armed party of them forced their way into the Viennese Chancellory and shot the Austrian Chancellor, Dollfuss, who was left to bleed slowly to death. They were successful in seizing the broadcasting station, from which they announced their coup to the nation, but the rest of the Austrian Cabinet reacted vigorously, the Austrian Army was loyal, and moreover Mussolini intervened. At that date the Italian dictator was not reconciled to his German imitator absorbing Austria and he sent three Italian divisions up to the Austrian border by the Brenner Pass. Germany at that time had little armed strength; indeed, as Mr. Muggeridge has pointed out, Hitler's greatest asset, then and even later, 'was the incredulity which his intentions aroused. They were so confused, seemed so fantastic . . .'. The rising of July 1934 was suppressed, but Hitler was by no means confused in his determination to overrun Austria as soon as he could.

On 16th March 1935 he announced that Germany repudiated those clauses of the Versailles Treaty which left her or were intended to leave her disarmed—the clauses Lord Grey had in mind when he had said on Hitler's accession two years earlier, 'The great security for peace at the present moment is that Germany is not armed, and not in a position to go to war.'[1] Now the German armed forces were again assured of a steady flow of conscripts —and on the same day military service in France was extended to two years. Hitler also openly boasted that his air force, which at that moment was not supposed to exist, was already equal in strength to that of Great Britain. But not only did Hitler reintroduce compulsory military service; the whole effort of education

[1] Lord Grey of Fallodon, as Sir Edward Grey, was Foreign Secretary in 1914.

in Germany, from infancy onwards, was directed towards producing a German who could with the minimum of additional
training be turned into a soldier.

The other dictator, Mussolini, was not without his own ambitions, and on 2nd October 1935, while the League of Nations
was endeavouring to settle a frontier incident at Wal Wal
between Italians and Abyssinians, the Italian Army began to in-
vade that unfortunate, primitive but ancient empire. As there
could be no question who was the aggressor, the League eventually decided to apply economic sanctions to Italy—that is, to exert
pressure by a refusal to trade. An exception was, however, made
in the case of oil, of which Italy has no indigenous supply and
which was one of the sinews of war she was obliged to import.[1]
The embargo did not apply to oil, but the supply of arms was
rigorously denied to both sides. The result was that the inhabitants of Abyssinia were practically reduced to defending themselves with spears, and the Italians were rapidly able to overcome
the resistance of their coloured antagonists by the use of tanks
and mustard gas poured on the unprotected tribesmen from the
air. The sanctions against Italy lingered on until terminated by
Mr. Neville Chamberlain, who termed them 'the very mid-
summer of madness'. Their only lasting effect was to alienate
Mussolini and still further discredit the League of Nations.
Mussolini's defiance of the League succeeded. Hitler drew his
own conclusions. 'In Japan,' wrote Mr. Winston Churchill,
'there were also pensive spectators.'

The year 1936 opened with the death of King George V, the
King who had seen the British Empire through the First World
War, and it also witnessed the startling abdication of his successor. The anxiety over the new King's marriage and the fear
that it might divide his peoples or endanger the position of the
monarchy not unnaturally diverted some attention from the continued series of unprepossessing events abroad. The most por-
tentous was Hitler's announcement on 7th March that his troops
were at that moment reoccupying the Rhineland zone which had

---

[1] It must be borne in mind that throughout this period the United States was not a
member of the League of Nations, so that the burden of leadership fell on Britain and
France alone, and France was still hoping to enrol Italy as an ally against Germany.

been demilitarised under the Versailles Treaty and that he proposed to start building fortifications along the frontier between Germany and France. With this frontier unfortified on the German side, French troops could enter the Rhineland almost at will. With the Western Wall, as Hitler called it, in existence, not only was this no longer the case, but troops would be free for adventures elsewhere—for instance, in Austria. Indeed the German Foreign Minister said on 18th May to the American Ambassador in Moscow: 'As soon as our fortifications are constructed and the countries in Central Europe realise that France cannot enter German territory, all these countries will begin to feel very differently about their foreign policies, and a new constellation will develop.'[1]

In France the Government's immediate proposal was to mobilise the armed forces. Indeed at that time France alone was amply strong enough to drive the fledgling German Army out of the Rhineland. Moreover, had France mobilised there is virtually no doubt in Churchill's view that Britain and France's allies in eastern Europe would have been obliged to do the same. In that case it can be almost certainly assumed, in the light of what we know to-day, that the German General Staff would have insisted on withdrawal. And if Hitler had been made to look ridiculous and had his bluff called at a time when he was still dependent on bluff, he might still have been clawed down from his seat of power by ambitious successors, and in the jungle which he had made of German politics have lost his life. After the middle of 1936 he was no longer dependent on bluff. It is notoriously easy to trace the 'ifs' of history with the wisdom of hindsight, but we do so because Sir Winston Churchill is insistent that at this point—if not indeed again still later—the Second World War might by courage have been averted.

France did not mobilise. Instead the French Ministers came to London, where they had discussions with Mr. Baldwin's Government, where they met counsels of restraint, dismay, delay and inaction. 'Clemenceau or Poincaré,' writes Churchill pugnaciously, 'would have left Mr. Baldwin no option.' But this was the

[1] Winston S. Churchill, *The Second World War*. Vol. 1: *The Gathering Storm* (Cassell, 2nd revised edn., 1949).

G

period of appeasement, of the sustained attempt, which we have still to trace, to buy the dictators off by giving them what they wanted, even at the expense of others. It was the period of the 'peace pledge', in which many young men (shortly to fight most gallantly) went on record that they were unwilling to take up arms for King and country; the period when the ghastly slaughter of the First World War left the peoples especially of Britain and France imbued with a longing for peace at any price. Mr. Baldwin said of the election in 1935—and no-one has denied Mr. Baldwin's ability to sense the mood of the electorate—that there was then 'probably a stronger pacifist feeling running in the country than at any time since the war'.

The old diplomacy had relied upon force: upon the delicate manipulation of force in the hands of experienced professional diplomats working in secret and aware that peace depended upon their achieving and maintaining a precarious balance. In this 'century of the common man' secrecy cannot be maintained; the delicate issues of diplomacy must be put before mass electorates, and thus can only be put crudely. The old diplomacy was not without its successes, but it did not avoid war and some means of doing so must be found if we are not to scorch ourselves and all conscious life from the surface of our planet. The problem of reducing the relations between sovereign nations to conformity with law and Christian conduct—or of finding a better substitute for sovereign nations—is the central problem of our age, and no solution is offered to it here. It is here only recorded that in the circumstances preceding the Second World War, as we now know them to have been, a greater willingness to employ force against the dictators would paradoxically have made war less likely.

Hitler, we now know, gambled on the unlikelihood of ever being faced by a coalition of all the major powers in the field together. Moreover, appeasement, continued in the absence of any conciliation on the other side—continued at the expense of principle—led to a moral deterioration, to a dull apathy, and at length begat a feeling of revulsion and shame, such that when in the end war came, it came to many almost as a relief. Mr. Muggeridge, writing while the mood was still fresh in recollection, says of this period: 'Considering the tenacity with which British interests and prestige had formerly been defended, it was surprising that now they should be so unresistingly sacrificed. Nerveless seemingly were the hands which exercised authority, feeble the response when authority was challenged.' And again: 'Parliament, reflecting the mood of those it represented, gave an impression of waiting–like the elderly inmates of a private hotel waiting for the post, though they have no particular reason for expecting a letter; or waiting for evening to come and the blinds to be drawn, though they have no particular reason for preferring evening to day. A strange apathy was apparent, occasionally broken when some event, exceptionally violent, impelled attention. Then for a little while voices were raised demanding an explanation, prophesying woe, pleading that it was still not too late if only at this eleventh hour. . . . Soon this clamour died away, and the old apathy returned; the waiting, no-one knew for what.'[1]

But we are still in 1936. Before the end of that year the drums of war were louder, and much nearer. In July civil war broke out in Spain. To prevent it spreading, twenty-seven nations agreed not to intervene or take sides, but to 'hold the ring' while the Spanish Army, backed by the Church, fought it out under the leadership of General Franco against the Liberal-Communist Government, with its main strength in the industrial centres of the north. Here already was ample warning that the dictators' pledge could not be made the currency of international agreement, for both promptly broke their word. Regular formations of the Italian Army were sent to Franco's aid under the guise of 'volunteers'–a technique with which we renewed our acquaintance when the Chinese went into Korea. Hitler also sent support, but chiefly technicians and material which the General Staff wished to test under actual war conditions. Neither dictator could resist boasting of the aid given to Franco and both countries' troops were received with ceremonial welcome on their triumphant return. Some aid was given to the other side by the French and the Russians. But this was not the only help received by the legitimate Government of Spain, despite the fact that owing to

[1] Malcolm Muggeridge, *op. cit.*

'non-intervention' it was unable to purchase arms abroad. The issue between the two sides was one that nagged at the minds and hearts of many young men of socialist views, for it seemed to them that Franco's challenge to Spain was but a bitter, small rehearsal of the dictators' challenge to the rest of us. Many young men there were whose nervous response to that challenge would not permit them to wait until it reached them at home, but who went out to meet it in Communist-organised international brigades of real volunteers. Thus there were some on both sides who were killed before their countries were involved in war, but they died for the same issues.

Franco's ships maintained something of a blockade along the coast of Loyalist Spain and one can still recall the enthusiasm when British merchant captains went through the blockade with food for beleaguered Bilbao. Here again Franco had help from his friends of like persuasion and at one time Italian submarines were almost waging covert war on British merchant shipping. This was stopped by some firm action on the part of Mr. Eden, already then Foreign Secretary, who brought about an agreement that the naval forces of the signatories to the non-intervention pact should jointly patrol the troubled waters and take any necessary action to protect neutral shipping—an agreement which it was apparent the Royal Navy could be relied upon to put into operation. In another respect the Spanish War also provided a rehearsal for what followed, for the little ancient Basque city of Guernica was destroyed by German bombers. It thus became the pathetic forerunner of Warsaw, Rotterdam, Belgrade, Dunkirk, Coventry, Stalingrad, and, in their turn, of Vienna, Cologne, Essen, Dresden, Berlin, Tokyo, Hiroshima and Nagasaki. In January 1939, after a major offensive carried out with the aid of strong German and Italian mechanised forces, General Franco burst through the starved Catalan army and occupied Barcelona. Hundreds of thousands of refugees and defeated militiamen struggled painfully into France, many fighting a continuous rearguard action and persistently bombed from the air.[1]

[1] The Spanish Civil War has given us the expression 'fifth column', meaning a body of sympathisers attacking one's enemy in the rear. It was first used by one of Franco's generals, who boasted that he had four columns converging on Madrid and a 'fifth column' of unknown supporters in the city itself ready to strike when the time came.

On 21st May 1936 Hitler solemnly declared in the Reichstag: 'Germany neither intends nor wishes to interfere in the internal affairs of Austria, to annex Austria, or to conclude an Anschluss' (union). On 11th July he signed a pact with the Austrian Government agreeing not to influence Austria's internal affairs, nor to support the Austrian Nazis. On 16th July secret instructions were sent to the Austrian Nazis to intensify their activities. In the same month the German General Staff was given the task of drawing up plans for the invasion of Austria at the appropriate time. During the following year, we now know, Hitler expounded his plans to his service chiefs. Germany must have more 'living space'. This would be gained by the extermination of other peoples in eastern Europe. It involved removing populations from Poland, White Russia and the Ukraine. War with England and France was inevitable, for they would not willingly accept a 'German Colossus' in the heart of Europe. Germany must therefore choose the most favourable opportunity and commence her war before her opponents were ready.

On 11th January 1938 President Roosevelt–deeply anxious on account of the international situation–proposed to invite Britain, France, Germany and Italy to a conference in Washington. Before doing so, however, he sought the views of the British Government in confidence. This was a major step and one which showed great political courage, when one remembers how strongly the U.S.A. was then opposed to any entanglement in European affairs. But Mr. Chamberlain, then Prime Minister, was afraid of offending the dictators. He felt that he was winning them over by being conciliatory, by removing every possible reasonable grievance; that he was building up a direct understanding with them which this conference would have imperilled. The American initiative was not grasped. 'That Mr. Chamberlain, with his limited outlook and inexperience of the European scene, should have possessed the self-sufficiency to wave away the proffered hand stretched out across the Atlantic leaves one, even at this date, breathless with amazement.' (The words, of course, are Sir Winston Churchill's.) This was the background of the resignation of Mr. Eden in February 1938 and of his under-secretary, Lord Cranborne. As the American initiative was still confidential, the ostensible reason for Mr. Eden's action was that he objected to our opening general discussions for an agreement with Italy while Mussolini still had five divisions of his army in Spain. 'We must not,' said Mr. Eden, 'buy goodwill.' Nevertheless Chamberlain's policy of trying to appease the dictators was supported by his Cabinet and military advisers.

On 12th February 1938 the Austrian Chancellor Schuschnigg was summoned to Hitler's Bavarian eyrie at Berchtesgaden. He was confronted with an ultimatum of which the terms were not open to discussion. The Austrian Nazi leader, Seyss-Inquart, was to join the Cabinet and the Austrian Nazi Party to be incorporated in the Government Party. The alternative was war. Schuschnigg capitulated, but on 9th March he announced that to strengthen his position he would hold a plebiscite on Sunday, the 13th. On the morning of the 11th Seyss-Inquart came to tell him that there had been a telephone call from Goering; the plebiscite must be called off, and he, Seyss-Inquart, nominated Chancellor within two hours. Schuschnigg resigned, but old President Miklas refused to appoint a Nazi in his place. The German Army accordingly carried out the plan drawn up in 1936 and invaded Austria. On 12th March Hitler announced that the Austrian state had ceased to exist and was incorporated in the German Reich. Sir Stafford Cripps then predicted in the House of Commons: 'The independence of Austria has disappeared . . . Germany's next act of aggression will be directed against Czechoslovakia and then the people of Britain will find themselves back in the days of 1914.'

We now know that on 28th May Hitler issued instructions for an attack to be mounted against Czechoslovakia as soon as he gave the word. His generals demurred, for France and Britain still disposed of a vastly superior strength, except in the air; the Western Wall was still incomplete; the Czech Army was efficient and Russia, well-disposed towards Czechoslovakia, was not to be ignored. Their view was that of the conscientious professional, Hitler's that of an inspired madman. He reassured Field-Marshal Keitel:'I will decide to take action against Czechoslovakia only if I am firmly convinced, as in the case of the demilitarised zone and the entry into Austria, that France will not march and that therefore England will not intervene.'[1] On 12th September the British Cabinet gave the French an inconclusive answer to *their* question–namely, whether, if Hitler attacked Czechoslovakia and France mobilised, Britain would do the same. On the 14th Chamberlain, without consulting his Cabinet, telegraphed to Hitler suggesting a personal visit. Next day the British Prime Minister flew to Munich and followed in Schuschnigg's footsteps on to Berchtesgaden.

He returned with the impression that Hitler was a man who kept his word, whose large but not impossible demands could be satisfied, and who might then be expected to preserve the peace. On the 19th the British and French Governments handed over to the Czechs an outline of the concessions which they deemed sufficient and recommended should be made–the cession to Germany of all areas containing a majority of people of German origin. At 2 a.m. on the night of 20th–21st September 1938 the British and French Ministers in Prague called on President Benes urging him to make this offer, and on the 21st the Czech Government complied. It issued a statement: 'You shall to-day level no reproaches at those who have forsaken us in our hour of direst need. History will pass judgement on the events of these days.'

The following day Chamberlain flew a second time to Germany, to reap the fruits of his mediation. He found Hitler dissatisfied and to his astonishment was given a memorandum containing a time limit for Czech evacuation of the Sudetenland–a document which Chamberlain described as an ultimatum rather than a memorandum. Meanwhile the Czechs were mobilising; there was also a partial call to arms in France, and on 28th September the British fleet was made ready for war. Meanwhile also General Beck, the Chief of the German Army General Staff, resigned because he disapproved so strongly of Hitler's gamble. There was, had we but known it, a plot among the senior officers of the German Army to remove Hitler at this point before he could plunge into what they considered the madness of a war for which they were not ready. Opinion in the

[1] International Military Tribunal, Nuremberg. Quoted Churchill, *The Second World War.*

higher ranks of the German Navy and Air Force was equally against Hitler.

At 3 p.m. on the 28th Chamberlain was giving the House of Commons a summary of what had transpired on his second visit to Germany when Lord Halifax, his new Foreign Secretary, passed him a message which had just been brought to the House. It was Hitler's invitation to Chamberlain, Mussolini and the French Premier, Daladier, to meet him at Munich. On the following day Chamberlain flew to Germany for the third time. What transpired at Munich was characterised by Mr. Churchill in his subsequent speech in the House of Commons in the words: 'The German Dictator, instead of snatching his victuals from the table, has been content to have them served to him course by course. £1 was demanded at the pistol's point. When it was given, £2 was demanded at the pistol's point. Finally, the Dictator consented to take £1 17s. 6d.' But this was not Chamberlain's view at the time. He was convinced that he had dragged peace out of the very jaws of war; that it was 'peace for our time' and also that it was 'peace with honour'. In their infinite relief after having had the hideous countenance of modern war suddenly thrust so close to them and then miraculously withdrawn, most of the Press and much of the public was also ecstatic with joy; indeed the *Daily Telegraph* had already written of Chamberlain's announcement of the Munich Conference that not Gladstone in his most compelling hour had ever won a triumph like that. But many there were who felt degraded and appalled, who questioned bitterly whether it was peace with honour, or whether indeed it was peace at all. And in Germany the generals who had considered Hitler's bluff the action of an irresponsible lunatic felt silly when it again succeeded. 'Thus,' writes Sir Winston Churchill, 'did Hitler finally become the undisputed master of Germany. . . .'

Next year, on 12th March, Germany occupied what remained of Czechoslovakia and the Czech state ceased to have any independent existence. This was the end of appeasement, for Mr. Chamberlain was a man with a hard moral core. He had been foolhardy in following his own 'hunch' in a sphere in which he was totally inexperienced and in taking the gravest decisions on his own responsibility against expert advice, but he had been led on only by his passionate desire for peace. Now at last he realised that this desire had been flattered merely to deceive him.

A week later the U.S.S.R. proposed a conference of the powers, but the suggestion was not taken up. Little has been said of the Russians in the above account. We know that Chamberlain regarded them with suspicion and as militarily unimportant, although the German General Staff did not share this view. Our general opinion of the Russian Army was low at the time, partly because of the great 'purge' which took place in January 1937, when not less than 5,000 officers and officials were murdered—those who were suspected of plotting to overthrow Stalin and to set up a new Government based on a policy of close co-operation with Germany. This had left the Soviet Army deficient in senior officers and it was also doubted how effectively Russia could bring aid to Czechoslovakia across the intervening barrier imposed by geography. Thus it came that Litvinov, the Foreign Commissar, was ignored when at the height of the Czech crisis he told the assembled League of Nations that he had assured the French: 'Our War Department is ready immediately to participate in a conference, with representatives of the French and Czechoslovak War Departments, in order to discuss the measures appropriate to the moment.' This was on 21st September 1938; he had further stated categorically that the U.S.S.R. was ready to go to the aid of Czechoslovakia in accordance with the Soviet-Czech Pact. Throughout the crisis Russia's massive bulk on the Eastern flank had been ignored.

On 5th April 1939 Italy started bombing Albanian towns without warning. By the 8th she had conquered that small, mountainous country, which was to serve as a passage to enable the Italians to get at Greece. On 26th April Mr. Chamberlain announced that all young men of 20 and 21 would be immediately conscripted for service with the armed forces. The beat of drums was now loud and insistent, drowning all the cheerful clatter of everyday life.

Early in May Litvinov, the Jew, ceased to be the Soviet Foreign Commissar and Molotov succeeded him. This marked the end

of Stalin's attempt to organise an eastern front against Hitler with the aid of Britain, France, Poland, Roumania, Finland and the Baltic states—all of whom, except the first two, had unfortunately in their history reason to fear Russia at least as much as Germany. The U.S.S.R. could no longer be ignored; the way was now open—since Hitler would no longer have to negotiate through a Jew—for a violent reversal of Soviet policy, such as would not have been possible in a democracy.

The Pact of Steel was signed between Italy and Germany on 22nd May. Next day Hitler explained to his Chiefs of Staff: 'It is a question of expanding our living space in the East and of securing our food supplies. There is therefore no question of sparing Poland, and we are left with the decision to attack Poland at the first suitable opportunity. We cannot expect a repetition of the Czech affair. There will be war.'[1] Ciano, Mussolini's son-in-law, notes in his diary for 11th August: 'The German decision to fight is implacable.' On 23rd August (while a British mission was also in Moscow to negotiate an alliance) a non-aggression pact was signed between Germany and the U.S.S.R., which, at any rate temporarily, safeguarded the German Army's eastern flank from any major attack. At dawn on 1st September the German Army invaded Poland and two days later was at war with the British Empire.

Mr. Churchill was called back to office and became First Lord of the Admiralty, the post he had occupied twenty-five years previously. Mr. Chamberlain remained Prime Minister, but his dry, narrow personality could not provide the leadership needed in the unequal struggle which lay ahead. Early in May 1940 he was obliged to listen while in the House of Commons Mr. Amery quoted at him the dreadful words used by Cromwell to the Long Parliament: 'You have sat too long here for any good you have been doing. Depart, I say, and let us have done with you. In the name of God, go!' Next day Mr. Lloyd George made his last decisive intervention in the House, an intervention heavy with the weight of his years and experience as Prime Minister in the First World War and afterwards at Versailles. He said of

[1] Quoted Churchill, *op. cit.*

Mr. Chamberlain: 'He has appealed for sacrifice . . . I say solemnly that the Prime Minister should give an example of sacrifice, because there is nothing that can contribute more to victory in this war than that he should sacrifice the seals of office.' On the tenth of that month Germany attacked France and Belgium and without warning and without cause invaded Holland on land and from the air, from across the frontier and by the use of 'fifth columnists' previously planted amongst the Dutch people, reducing much of almost defenceless Rotterdam to rubble. The Dutch Ministers flew to London. The same day Mr. Churchill became Prime Minister.

At this dramatic moment there thus came to power a man whose own sense of the dramatic has always been keen, and who by birth and ability, training, experience and interest was shaped and moulded for this supreme test. Sir Winston himself always believed in his destiny; that his several escapes from imminent death have been that he might serve a later purpose. Born, by the accident of a premature appearance, in Blenheim Palace, he was imbued with the tradition of its builder, the great Duke of Marlborough, Captain-General of Her Majesty's armies, leader of the victorious coalition which rescued Europe from the ambitions of Louis XIV. Churchill was steeped in the details of Marlborough's campaigns, and had visited every battlefield in writing the life of his great ancestor. Moreover, his mother was American and he thus also exemplified in his own flesh the alliance of the English-speaking peoples on which victory was to depend.

The study of the art of war was in fact a lifelong interest: at the age of 14 he was staging well-conceived manœuvres with an army of 500 lead soldiers. In the First World War he actually begged the Prime Minister to relieve him of his appointment as First Lord of the Admiralty, so that he might seek the military glory for which he craved as a commander in the field. When restored to office in 1917 as Minister of Munitions—but not to the Cabinet—he tells us that he 'managed to be present at nearly every important battle during the rest of the war'. To him war was an art to which its practitioners should bring high seriousness —he was never careless of lives lost or broken—skill, imagination, and ebullient spirits. All this indeed is apparent from the handling of operations on our side.

Here then was a brilliant, rapid mind, of extraordinary energy and drive, not gladly suffering fools, seeing issues in clear black and white (which makes it so much easier to take action on them), readily dramatising them in terms of good and evil with himself as champion of the good.[1] Yet in the public eye he seemed an unstable character, his formidable ability driven on by an overweaning ambition; there was doubt as to whether he would have the necessary staying power when 'the gallop of high spirits has run its course'. Asquith, when Prime Minister, often referred to him as 'my right honourable and picturesque colleague'. He lost office in 1915 over the Dardanelles, suffered agonies of frustration and discouragement until it was regained in 1917, lost it again between 1922 and 1924 when he changed parties. Between 1929, when the Conservative administration was defeated by Labour, and 1939, when he was again appointed First Lord, he was in the political wilderness, his public career apparently at an end. Ramsay MacDonald, Baldwin, Neville Chamberlain were all equally unwilling to have this explosive force in their humdrum administration. There is no ready parallel to his undaunted persistence in those ten years—unsupported by any party and derided by most politicians—in trying to save his country from war by what we now know to have been remarkable foresight.

In 1940 the man who had first become a Cabinet Minister in 1908, but whose career had seemed finished, suddenly became Prime Minister. 'As I went to bed at about 3 a.m. I was conscious of a profound sense of relief. At last I had authority to give directions over the whole scene.' The Chiefs of Staff, instead of reporting to their own Ministers (Admiralty, War, Air), reported direct to him. The Joint Planning Committee of the three

---

[1] Is it not characteristic that in another context he has written: 'I cannot pretend to feel impartial about the colours. I rejoice with the brilliant ones, and I am genuinely sorry for the poor browns. When I get to heaven I mean to spend a considerable proportion of my first million years in painting, and so get to the bottom of the subject. But then I shall require a still gayer palette than I get here below. I expect orange and vermilion will be the darkest, dullest colours upon it, and beyond them will be a whole range of wonderful new colours which will delight the celestial eye'—*Thoughts and Adventures*.

Services worked directly under him as Minister of Defence. So he became, subject always to the continuing support of Parliament, almost a dictator in the daily conduct of the war—but a dictator whose administration was free from the staggering inefficiencies and muddles, the corruption and personal struggles amongst the henchmen, which we now know flourished under Hitler and Mussolini. The mistakes of the First World War were not repeated here. Lloyd George had struggled in vain with his generals to prevent the holocaust of Passchendaele, had even felt himself driven to the dangerous expedient of holding back reserves under his own hand in England, lest they should be thrown away by the commanders in France. This time the generals were firmly under civilian control—but what a civilian! General Eisenhower testifies: '. . . Mr. Churchill always participated with the British Chiefs in the formation and despatch of instructions, even those that were strictly military, sometimes only tactical, in character.'[1] In the past his pugnacious self-confidence, his impulsive energy, his fertility of ideas and frank ambition had threatened to overwhelm his colleagues and had made him suspect to his plain countrymen. The Second World War provided a sufficiently heavy flywheel or 'governor' on his native ebullience. The task was adequate to the man—and humanity rejoices to-day that the man was equal to the task.

Once again we make no attempt to describe the different campaigns of the war. On this occasion there could be no period of siege warfare in France; no monotonous, slogging slaughter. Nor is it at all easy to summarise the phases of this Second War, for the struggle developed in a complex pattern all over the globe, with the Far East—in the First War a minor theatre—almost equally involved with the West. At the one extreme submarines stalked each other in the cold darkness of the sea and at the other Hitler's latest engines of war penetrated the stratosphere. Three technical features strongly differentiated this from previous wars. One was the impulsive rush of armoured formations supported from the air, for both the tank and the aeroplane, infants in 1918, had now reached maturity. At first Germany's overwhelming preponderance carried her right across France; later on, in Russia, in

[1] *Crusade in Europe* (Heinemann, 1949).

North Africa and again in western Europe, the tank battle developed into a clash of equal mastodons. The rapid manœuvre of armour and aircraft, the intimate co-operation of both with infantry and artillery were made possible by the perfection of wireless, which at the other end of the scale permitted the control and conduct of vast and intricate operations over great distances and the flow of information without which such control is impossible. But wireless was only the first of the progeny of electronics. There was radar to detect hostile aircraft, invisible ships and submarines; eventually radar to guide the bomber and the opposing fighter on to the target and to sight the gun. At the end of the war there were already the proximity fuse, the pilotless aircraft (the V1), the rocket (V2) and the guided missile, precursor of to-day's self-guiding missile. Nor should we forget the sudden menace presented by Hitler's magnetic mine at the beginning of the war.

From the beginning also, in daylight hostile aircraft could swoop hawklike on any movement on land or in the narrow seas. Great naval battles, such as those in the Coral Sea and off Midway Island, were fought by ships invisible to each other over the curve of the horizon, but sending out their carrier-based aircraft. Submarines and capital ships alike were chased and bombed or torpedoed from the air. Armies could be pinned down by day as the French in 1940 or their communications totally disrupted like those of the Germans in France four years later. Armed men could be suddenly dropped from the sky, or heroic individuals secretly deposited and collected. Troops were supplied from the air and whole formations picked up and dropped elsewhere, as demonstrated by the XIVth Army in Burma. And from the air the war was literally carried home to the civilians, tons of high explosive and phosphorous thrown down night after night on cities, civilians little safer than soldiers, acres of dwellings destroyed, industry hampered. In Britain 60,000 civilians were killed–a modest figure compare to our enemy's–as against 1,400 in 1914–18.

In the first phase of the land fighting Germany occupied the whole northern coast-line of Europe from the North Cape to the Pyrenees. The British Expeditionary Force was miraculously extricated at Dunkirk, but after June 1940 we were left alone, almost disarmed, awaiting invasion. Hitler's task was to ferry the heavy striking power of an army—what could not be carried by air—in the face of the Royal Navy, across that vital ditch the English Channel. If his bombers could dominate the air, they could hunt the ships crawling like beetles on the surface of the sea; but bombers in their turn are slow pigeons to the fierce hawklike attack of fighters and he must therefore first destroy the British fighters. It is a matter of history that in the Battle of Britain the German Air Force was decisively defeated.

In June 1941 Hitler suicidally invaded Russia and in a famous speech Mr. Churchill, no friend of Soviet Russia for twenty years past, immediately acclaimed the U.S.S.R. our ally, for, as he remarked privately, if Hitler invaded Hell it would be desirable to find something friendly to say about the Devil.[1] On 7th December 1941, while the Japanese emissary was negotiating certain points of dispute in Washington, wave after wave of Japanese carrier-borne aircraft suddenly attacked and destroyed the American Pacific Fleet in Pearl Harbour. Almost immediately afterwards Germany and Italy declared war on the U.S.A. After 1941 we were no longer alone, for vast powers were stirring on our side.

In May 1942 the U.S.A. defeated the Japanese Navy and checked her further seaborne expansion. In October Rommel was defeated in Africa at El Alamein. In November the German Sixth Army was desperately trying to cross the Volga at Stalingrad to turn the Russian flank. After being rigidly extended far too long in the prong of a salient by Hitler's fanatical obstinacy it was encircled by the Russians and destroyed. The tide had turned. May 1943 saw the end of the fighting in North Africa, July the Allied landing in Sicily, followed at once by our clawing a hold on the Italian mainland. This was the beginning of the way back, the return to the European mainland. The Anglo-American seaborne assault on the coast of Normandy took place in June 1944. A year later Hitler's enemies advancing from east and west covered the surface of Germany as the waters cover the sea.

[1] The remark is mentioned in his war memoirs.

The scattered Japanese forces were not separately reduced, for the Americans struck at the homeland. On 6th August 1945 an atom bomb was dropped on Hiroshima destroying 80,000 people immediately[1] and on 9th August another on Nagasaki. They initiate a new epoch in the history of human beings.

[1] Ultimately about a quarter of a million people lost their lives as a result of the bomb and of the radio-activity, fire and disruption it caused.

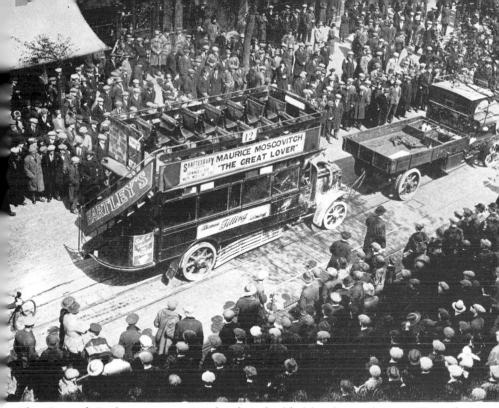

. The General Strike, 1926: a London bus disabled by the strikers. (The volunteer driver generally had a policeman on the seat beside him and the bonnet was often tied up with barbed wire to prevent damage to the engine.) . *(Picture Post Library)*

. 1932: ''dole'' queue outside a Clydeside Labour Exchange. *(Associated Newspapers)*

Exclusive News Agenc

9. Hero-worship: Hitler about 1936.

10. Procession in honour of Mao Tse Tung, founder of the Chinese People's Republic.

Camera Pres

8

The World To-day

(i)

'We were not aware that civilisation was a thin and
precarious crust.'

J. M. KEYNES

THIS is on the whole an unpleasant book, and we come now
to its most unpleasant part; but to be honest some reference
to the moral breakdown of the period seems inescapable.
Modern man believes that life is sacred. Every individual has an
equal claim to the fullest development of his native faculties;
slavery was abolished more than a hundred years ago and it is a
crime to put an end to the life even of those who are mortally
sick and suffering. In war, very well, the preservation of liberty
ranks above that of life, but in peace life is sacred and liberty of
person and conscience is entrenched in the rule of law, buttressed
by democratic procedure. This is the legacy of past generations.
How then do we explain the sudden regression to totalitarianism,
the refusal to be bound by treaties, the attempt—for which history
has no comparable precedent—to exterminate a whole people,
the return of slavery on a vast scale and the use of torture?

Here we have a succinct description of the essential characteristics of the dictatorships of Mussolini and Hitler, and of the
anti-democratic parties which helped them to power: 'Having
exploited every difficulty of the parliamentary governments and
every popular grievance, the parties succeeded—amid some show
of violence—in gaining power with constitutional formalities. The
real fascist revolutions followed, and like the Bolshevik Revolution were carried out by a party which already controlled all the
power mechanisms of the state. Police and army were reinforced
by secret police and party militias, and were used to crush every
form of opposition. A reign of terror was instituted whilst the

party consolidated its grip. And the party, having served so well as the agency for effecting revolution, was preserved (after due purging) as the instrument of the new tyranny. Disciplined, centralised, indoctrinated, privileged, it occupied all the key positions in the state and in national life. Thus it became possible to have not only absolute power but totalitarian power, for no limits were admitted to the scope of state competence. Churches were reduced to political impotence, free trade unions destroyed and strikes forbidden, free associations demolished or absorbed. Every agency for moulding public opinion—the schools, the press, radio, cinema, public meetings—was taken under party control. No element of social life was accepted as lying beyond the direction of the government. Never before in the history of the world had ruthless men enjoyed such complete and far-reaching power over the lives of millions. Former dictators, if equally absolute, had not been equally totalitarian in their aims. The fascist dictators combined the hysterical mass appeal of a Robespierre with the powerful governmental machinery of a Napoleon, and added to both the whole repertoire of devices which tend to increase the power of any modern government: the machine-gun, scientific taxation, and efficient civil-service.'[1] Democracy had been regarded as the final stage in the advance and development of government, but by 1939 every one of the Balkan states whose boundaries had been so hopefully defined after the Great War had relapsed into some form of dictatorship.

In Hitler's Germany liberals and Jews (Hitler's definition included a number who were not of the Jewish faith) were imprisoned in 'concentration camps'—hutted prisons in which the brutality of the guards was unchecked by law; an institution which our Victorian grandparents would have regarded with horrified incredulity, but one which has become a familiar idea to us. The Jews were vilified in Nazi Germany, excluded from social and business life and systematically despoiled. But worse was to follow. '. . . We possess the minutes of an important conference of Nazi officials (in January 1942) . . . in which it was decided, in the expectation of victory, to complete the annihilation of the 11 million Jews whom the Nazis calculated that they

---

[1] David Thomson, *World History from 1914 to 1950* (Oxford, 1954).

would be able to reach. . . . In the meantime the policy of extermination was extended . . . to all Jews already within the Nazis' clutches. It was for them that the additional death camps in Poland were devised; and all through 1942 and 1943 transports were being sent eastwards and northwards from France, Belgium and Holland, from Germany, Austria and Czechoslovakia, from Hungary and the Balkans. At Auschwitz it was possible to kill 2,000 people in a single operation lasting but a quarter of an hour, and to repeat this three or four times a day. . . . How summary was the dispatch with which arrivals were treated is revealed by the story of a train-load of Germans evacuated from Hamburg who had been sent to Lwow to make their homes there. They were seized, stripped of their possessions, and gassed by the Gestapo, before it was discovered that they were not Jews. . . . In the camp of Auschwitz alone it is reported by the Nazi commandant himself that $2\frac{1}{2}$ million persons . . . were gassed, and that another half-million died of starvation and disease.'[1]

In Soviet Russia concentration camps provided forced labour to aid the country's rapid industrialisation and for such undertakings as the White Sea Canal. Estimates of the amount of slave labour at one time employed by the Russian state vary between 7 and 15 million persons. Before Khrushchev decided to close these camps a great part of the industrialisation and opening up of Siberia was undertaken under police direction by those who were not free to go elsewhere, the N.K.V.D.

[1] *Survey of International Affairs 1939–1946: Hitler's Europe*, edited for the Royal Institute of International Affairs by Prof. Arnold and Veronica M. Toynbee (Oxford, 1954).
    Of the 12,000 Russian prisoners of war who built the huts and gas chambers of Auschwitz concentration camp about 450 survived. Perhaps we may quote very briefly from a remarkable article 'Dachau Revisited' by the Hon. Terence Prittie which appeared in the *Manchester Guardian* in December 1954: 'The new crematorium is labelled "Building 243A". Its doors are kept always open, for it is a museum of misery. It contains five main rooms, the first small and empty. Empty, that is, save for the thousands of names and messages scribbled on its bare walls. They are accompanied often by a cross, a pierced heart, or the Star of David. There are little messages—"Les Soissonais à leurs Martyrs", "Stanley Joachimiak was here K.Z. Dachau 1941–1945".
    'Beyond this room are the ovens, a big double oven flanked by two single ones and all three transformed into shrines. On them hang the flags of many nations, tattered vestments which have presumably been handed down from the churches that functioned in the camp, pine and laurel wreaths on nails. Some of them carry messages, "A nos morts", "Aux chers disparus". A bronze plaque has been let into one oven, bearing the names of the Brothers Vaarwel, of Antwerp.'

(secret police) being the country's biggest employers. Considerable numbers of German prisoners of war were used for at least ten years after the war.

The Germans themselves only adopted the expedient of forced labour under the pressure of war, and particularly after the labour crisis of the winter 1941–2. During 1942 the whole of occupied Europe was scoured for fresh labour and millions were transported to German factories–in places 'a regular manhunt was inaugurated',[1] men, women and adolescents being seized on the streets; of the 5 million foreign workers who went to Germany less than 200,000 went voluntarily. Their treatment varied according to their origin and their skill. All were treated badly and inadequately fed; the worst off (people from occupied eastern Europe) were treated as slaves. Under the pressure of war the concentration camps were also called upon to supply workers, and we have the memorandum of a remarkable agreement reached on 18th September 1942 between Himmler (Reichsfuehrer S.S. and chief of the Gestapo, or secret police) and the Minister of Justice, Thierack: 'Anti-social persons, instead of carrying out their sentences, will be handed over to the Reichsfuehrer S.S. to be worked to death. Persons under protective arrest, Jews, gypsies, Russians and Ukrainians, Poles with longer than three-year sentences, Czechs and Germans with longer than eight-year sentences, will all be handed over in accordance with decisions taken by the Reich Minister for Justice.'[2]

It is estimated that 6 million Jews were killed. If we want the total number of people killed in our period by man's inhumanity to man, we must add together the 10 million soldiers who died in the First World War; the 15.1 million nationals of countries west of the present boundaries of the U.S.S.R. who perished in the Second War–9 million of them civilians; the total, unverifiable, but put at 20 million, of Russian casualties in the Second War; the losses of the British Commonwealth, the 325,000 casualties of the U.S.A. and the 1½ million approximately suffered by Japan, of whom 330,000 were civilians killed

---

[1] International Military Tribunal, Nuremberg. Evidence of German officials. Quoted in *Hitler's Europe*.
[2] I.M.T., Nuremberg.

in air-raids. The total is far from complete, because we have omitted the numberless victims of the long wars in China, of the Spanish and Abyssinian wars, of the Russian terror and famine, while the Chinese Communist Government has stated that $2\frac{1}{4}$ million 'enemies of the people' have already perished at its hands. The most accurate attempt to assess population changes caused by the war in Europe is probably that of G. Frumkin, who calculates that the *military* losses of countries occupied by the German armies totalled 1,356,000, to which must be added about 4,254,000 non-Jewish civilians and 4,372,000 Jews–significant proportions as between military and civilian.[1] Perhaps it is enough for us to note that such has been the holocaust that we do not know how many human beings have perished even to the nearest million.

But not all are at rest. Millions more were uprooted from their homes and survived as refugees. 'In the aftermath of two world wars and a division of the earth between two blocks of powers the refugee is tending to become a permanent feature of the landscape. . . . a refugee is invariably and essentially someone who is homeless, uprooted; a helpless casualty, diminished in all his circumstances, the victim of events for which, at least as an individual, he cannot be held responsible.'

He often arrives 'as an individual without identity, papers or passport–and usually too without money. He has crossed, clandestinely, one or more frontiers, and has, on arrival, no valid residence permit; not being authorised to live in the country, *a fortiori* he has no right to work there. In some countries he can neither marry nor divorce nor inherit property. He might perhaps emigrate, but for that he needs a valid passport and the price of his fare. Very often, having neither house nor work, nor means of support, he may count himself lucky if he is put into a camp. There he waits weeks, months, even years, for his future to be decided, until some country or other agrees to take him. Even if the reception country grants him a residence permit– nearly always temporary–and a work permit, he will live in constant fear of losing this privilege, for he knows that it often needs

---

[1] *Population Changes* (Allen & Unwin, 1951). Many of the above figures are taken from the calculations of this experienced statistician.

little–an unfavourable police report–for him to be expelled, and to be liable to imprisonment because no other country will take him.'[1]

After the First World War there were over a million refugees; some who had fled from the Bolsheviks in Russia, some from the Turks in Armenia. Between 1937 and 1939 about 400,000 Spaniards crossed the Pyrenees into France; in May 1939 there were 401,000 Jewish refugees from Germany, Austria and those parts of Czechoslovakia already invaded by the Nazis. That was the position in 1939. When the fog of war began to lift slowly in the autumn of 1945 it revealed millions of prisoners estranged from their homes, millions who had been carried from the east, the west and the north of Europe to work in German factories and were now trying to make their way back through the armies and along the shattered lines of communication, millions more who had fled before hostile advancing armies or the fury of the bombing. Europe was like an ant-heap which has been stamped on. Moreover, as soon as the fighting was over the governments of both Czechoslovakia and Poland proceeded to expel all Germans from their territories. Between 5 and 6 million were uprooted from Poland and 2,700,000 from Czechoslovakia. Thousands also crowded into shattered Germany from Hungary, Roumania and Yugoslavia.

The number of Hungarians in Germany and Austria was between 800,000 and 1 million and there were also about 2 million 'displaced persons' of Ukrainian origin in the Western occupation zones of Germany: prisoners, survivors of forced labour, those who had fled before the Russians. Several million Poles were torn from their homes when their country became a battlefield. Of them over 5 million lost their lives in concentration camps, over 1 million were interned in the U.S.S.R.; 2½ million were deported to Germany. Some were forcibly enlisted into the German armed forces–about 150,000 prisoners of war were later liberated from the Germans by the Allies; some fled westwards from the Soviets in 1944–5. '. . . lastly, a mass of civilians, including many women and children, who were evacuated from the U.S.S.R.

---

[1] Jacques Vernant, *The Refugee in the Post-War World*–an account sponsored by the United Nations Commissioner for Refugees (Allen & Unwin, 1953).

across the Caucasus and Iran (Persia) and are now scattered throughout the Near East, East Africa and Asia.'[1] (Some of these last were subsequently resettled in Britain.)

Into this ant-heap of human misery and frustration the officials of the United Nations endeavoured to bring order and hygiene (it is a major medical triumph that there was no epidemic), to keep alive hope and ultimately to justify it, to bring back faith and charity to places from which they had been banished. They endeavoured also through an international search organisation to find the parents of the many thousands of children who were discovered living without any close relatives or legal guardian. Some had been evacuated from the bombing, some imported for labour, some separated from their families by the hazards of war, some deliberately abducted. Ten years later an international organisation was still caring for some 80,000 displaced persons in hutments in Germany.

But the tale is not yet done. During the period between April 1948 and February 1949 there was fighting between the Arab and Israeli armies. It culminated in the establishment of most of Palestine as a Jewish (Israeli) state, a national home for the survivors of persecution. It also caused the expulsion of 900,000 Arabs as completely destitute refugees. International relief has saved them from starvation, but the long years of waiting are destroying their hope of ever living normal lives again. Farther east, on 15th August 1947, the Indian Empire split into the Union of India and the Moslem state of Pakistan. It had been foreseen that minorities on either side might want to migrate and it was anticipated that such transfers, although not encouraged, could be effected peacefully, under control, and within relatively small areas. But the division of the erstwhile Empire gave the impression to the multitudes that the Hindus would become absolute masters on the one side of the new dividing line, the Moslems on the other. There was a sudden outburst of irrational mob passion, and the situation became immediately uncontrollable. Persecuted minorities fled *en masse* from their burning towns and villages; thousands were slaughtered. The exodus across great distances was painful in the extreme—many died on the way. The movement,

[1] Vernant, *op. cit.*, from which these figures are taken.

moreover, was infinitely more widespread than had been anticipated by the most pessimistic. 'Taken as a whole it is one of the
biggest migrations our era has known, perhaps the biggest of all
times.'[1] About 16 million human beings were uprooted. The
new governments had to settle 6,650,000 refugees in West
Pakistan and 800,000 in East Pakistan; 8,500,000 Hindus had
fled into the new state of India.

The Korean War broke out in 1950. South Korea now supports
about 5½ million refugees–a high proportion to a population
which in 1947 was estimated at a little under 19½ million. Of
the Korean refugee M. Vernant writes: 'He passes his days without any deep comprehension of the circumstances which have
made his home a battlefield and his liberation (from the Japanese)
a struggle. There is no bitterness, but considerable dejection.
Uprooted, penniless and bewildered, he does not indulge in re-
crimination, nor does he seek a panacea for his ills. He asks only
to continue to live peacefully his life of unremitting toil; for
he knows no other.'

'When it was all over Torture and Cannibalism were the
only two expedients that the civilised, scientific, Christian states
had been able to deny themselves. . . .' Thus Mr. Churchill,
summing up his account of the First World War. To complete
our tale of moral decline we must reluctantly admit that the police
of totalitarian states have not hesitated to use torture and the
Chinese also employed it to break the spirit of Western soldiers
captured in Korea. There remains now only cannibalism. Yet the
picture is not all darkness, for the constancy and heroism which
ordinary men have shown over long periods in these conditions
is beyond all ordinary praise. Indeed the devotion of soldiers and
often of the civilians on all sides to the causes which they have
espoused is ample evidence that the human spirit has not lost its
capacity for selflessness.

(ii)

'. . . the public mind in India may expand under our system until it has outgrown
our system . . . it will be the proudest day in English history.' MACAULAY in 1835

While some countries have retreated from liberal ideals others
have pushed them forward. It will surely be Earl Attlee's great

[1] Vernant, op. cit.

claim to an honourable place in history that it was his Government which, despite the preoccupations and weakness of the
immediate post-war period, completed the long, slow process
which gave self-government to the Indian peoples. The resurgence
of Asia and Africa, the end of the white man's domination over
the coloured, is one of the revolutionary changes of our time. The
story of Europe's relations with Asia is an astonishing and romantic one, but it is unfamiliar to most of us except for the bits and
pieces which find their way into the school history books to
illustrate the expansion of the British Empire. We can begin the
story with the arrival of Vasco da Gama in Calicut on the western
coast of India in 1498, and its first period, from then until about
1750, is one of exploration and expansion. It is a period of hardy
seafaring adventurers–Portuguese, Spanish, Dutch, then French
and English–establishing small trading posts–Muscat, Goa, Mal-
acca, Macao, Manila, Amboyna, Pondicherry, Bombay, Madras,
Calcutta–on little islands or on the coast, for the European power
was seaborne. It was chiefly spices and later tea which these
adventurers sought, ivory, perfumes and silk. They skirmished or
made treaties with the existing Asiatic rulers, such as the Mogul
emperors of India, upon whose affairs they impinged only at the
periphery, rather like flies vaguely apprehended on the hide of
an elephant. Thus it was that in 1715 the East India Company
obtained the permission of the Chinese Imperial Commissioner
for Trade to establish a permanent trading post in Canton,
although the 'Celestial Empire' did not allow the barbarian
foreigners to use sedan chairs, to row for pleasure on the river
or to visit a pleasure garden except under the charge of a petty
official.

The next is the period of conquest, for the Europeans began to
take sides in the internal affairs of the Asiatic states and, by
negotiation, force and occasionally fraud, established themselves
as rulers over large inland areas. It is now that Britain begins to
play the decisive part, for her strength in India made her a great
Asiatic power. This enabled her to force open the reluctant doors
of China against the will of the Manchu emperors, to make Europe
predominant in the Yangtze valley and to take the lead in con-

verting the rest of Asia into a European dependency. It is the period when British seaborne power is unquestioned and unassailable around the inhabited circumference of the globe. In 1842 the Treaty of Nanking gave Hong Kong to Britain and opened five Chinese ports 'where the foreign merchants with their families and establishments shall be allowed to reside for the purpose of carrying on their mercantile pursuits, without molestation or restraint'. These five ports were soon multiplied and spread not only over the entire coast but also included towns on the Yangtze stretching nearly a thousand miles upstream into the heart of China. There were British, French, German and Russian settlements. Nor were the Europeans content to be foreigners, hospitably if reluctantly quartered on Chinese soil; they went farther and established the principle of extra-territoriality. By this they introduced their own system of law into their settlements, refusing to submit to that of their hosts, so that in a few years all over China there were parcels of territory from which Chinese authority was excluded.

If the period from the middle of the eighteenth to the mid-nineteenth century may be called the period of conquest, that from 1850 to 1914 was that of European ascendancy in the East. Its beginning is perhaps best marked by the Treaty of Tientsin in 1858, which permitted Britain, and, following her, the other Great Powers, to maintain their ships of war in Chinese ports and on the Canton and Yangtze rivers so that a distance of 1,500 miles, right across the heart of China, was under the control of foreigners. Britain maintained a Rear-Admiral Yangtze. Between 1865 and 1885 missionaries penetrated into the farthest parts of China, taking their extra-territoriality with them. As late as 1870 the president of the Hong Kong Chamber of Commerce maintained that 'China can in no sense be considered a country entitled to all the same rights and privileges as civilised nations which are bound by international law'. By 1899 the Yunnan and the area bordering Indo-China were a French sphere of influence, Canton and the Yangtze and all the large area between a British sphere; Russia had a foothold in Manchuria, Germany in Kiao-chow and Shantung, Japan in Fukien. The railways intersecting the country were controlled by foreigners, the administration of the customs and salt taxes in European hands. At this point the United States, having occupied the Philippines and become a Pacific power, declared what became known as the 'open-door policy', to the effect that claims to spheres of influence should not be operated so as to limit free competition or damage the interests of other countries.

The Son of Heaven on the Dragon Throne of China had remained aloof from the 'Western chieftains' as long as he could. The Japanese were clear from the beginning that the only hope of resisting the Western barbarian lay in learning his military secrets—which they did, and put them to good use. The ships of Commodore Perry of the U.S. Navy broke Japan's long isolation in July 1853. After 1868 there were at one time as many as 5,000 foreigners in official employment in Japan, 1,300 of them in high positions. 'To wear foreign style clothes and leather shoes was now correct . . . of course few Japanese in 1875 or thereabouts could afford a complete foreign wardrobe, but it was usual to wear one or two articles of foreign clothing. Some interesting combinations were thus devised, such as a kimono over trousers, or a broad-cloth frock coat and a silk divided skirt with two swords in a sword belt. . . . The state of affairs is best illustrated by a song composed for children in 1878. It is called the Civilisation Ball Song and was designed to impress on young minds the advantages of Western culture. They were to count the bounces of the ball by reciting the names of ten objects deemed to be most worthy of adoption, namely gas lamps, steam engines, etc.'[1] The Japanese policy was fully justified by its results. By 1902 extraterritoriality was a thing of the past in Japan and she was allied to Britain as a Great Power in her own right.

British India developed from a colony, a possession, into an empire, with interests of its own and with a Civil Service conscious of a loyalty to the coloured millions in its care which sometimes brought it into conflict with the interests of British trade or imperialism. After 1875 British India began herself to expand

[1] Sir George Sansom, *The Western World and Japan*, quoted in K. M. Panikkar, *Asia and Western Dominance* (Allen & Unwin, 1953), whose analysis of the different periods in East-West relations is summarised here.

into other countries, occupying Burma and Baluchistan, establishing her influence in Afghanistan, and her authority from Aden to Hong Kong. This was the result of a partnership between the middle-class Britons in India and the Indian manpower which they organised. Moreover, the empire they established was based on Indian not British needs; it was Indian not British emigrants who swarmed into the newly annexed provinces.

The First World War brought Indian and Indo-Chinese troops to the aid of Britain and France in Europe. What they saw of the fighting was not calculated to raise their opinion of their white rulers, but their sojourn in Europe did give them ideas of democratic self-government. (Among the Chinese who went to France at the time was young Chou En-lai, who had to be expelled from the Chinese Labour Corps on account of the communistic notions he picked up, and is now able to put into practice as Prime Minister of the People's Republic of China.) At the critical point of the U-boat campaign in 1917 the Royal Navy, stretched to the utmost of its capacity, reluctantly consented to Japan being asked, as an ally, to send naval forces into the Mediterranean. After the war President Wilson's principle of self-determination for the countries of Europe was naturally read in the East as self-government for the coloured colonies of the European powers. The Western peoples themselves were thinking along the same lines, for we had lost faith in ourselves and in the white man's mission to rule the coloured man. The self-confident certainties of Kipling's day had become the subject of rather embarrassed ridicule in a period of socialist governments. Even in China the day had passed when British interests were not allowed to suffer on account of Chinese objections 'which a few gunboats . . . would overrule by the discharge of a few mortars'—to quote an article from the *China Repository* of ninety years earlier. After 1918 the flood of Western dominance was on the ebb and the European nations began to withdraw from Chinese concession ports.

In Afghanistan King Amanullah threw off British restrictions on his sovereignty and brought his remote country into the League of Nations as an independent state. That remarkable and widely travelled king Chulalongkorn (subject of the romantic play

The King and I) had throughout managed to maintain the independence of Siam by subtly playing off the British on his west against the French on his east. The Dutch had been firmly established in the Dutch East Indies and had been running Java as a plantation since 1760, but after 1908 a new Moslem Party, Sarekat Islam, took the lead in demanding independent nationhood—and despite its religious appeal was influenced by Communist doctrines. In Indo-China, where the French had been firmly established since their treaty of 1874, those who demanded independence were stimulated by three events in particular: the ease with which the Japanese had defeated Imperial Russia in the Russo-Japanese war of 1904–5, the success of the revolution which overthrew the Chinese Emperor in 1911, and the reforms of 1919 pointing towards self-government for India. It was, of course, the sensational, if short-lived defeat of the white governments by the Japanese in the Second World War which finally weakened the position of the British in Burma, of the Dutch in what since their withdrawal is called Indonesia and of the French in Indo-China. This country, now called Vietnam, is also divided into a Communist north and a southern part in which America, desperately sustaining a government with little hold on its suffering people is also trying to stem the Communist advance as it did in Korea.

After 1919 the process of British withdrawal was continuous in India, with the Indian National Congress forcing the pace. In Mahatma Gandhi the Indians produced not only a holy man in their own tradition but the inventor of a new political technique. Gandhi argued that British authority was in the last resort based on the co-operation of the Indian people. If that co-operation were withdrawn—without violence, for that is contrary to the tradition, but equally without yielding to force—then British authority must come to an end. Only a man who has completely mastered himself can successfully oppose passive non-co-operation to force (and probably only in India and in the Society of Friends are sufficient such men and women to be found). The struggle, moreover, was conducted within limits set by the moral code of the British Government, which did not apply force beyond the periodical imprisonment of the Congress leaders. Thirty-five years after the solemn and gorgeous ceremony in Delhi which marked the coronation of King George V as Emperor of India the Union Jack was lowered in that historic city. In August 1947 the last British troops voluntarily left India and brought to an honourable close the chapter of history which opened with the Battle of Plassey in 1757. Burma became an independent republic. India, Pakistan, Ceylon, Ghana, Nigeria, Sierra Leone, little Gambia, Kenya, Uganda, Tanzania (the union of Tanganyika and Zanzibar), Zambia (previously Northern Rhodesia), Malawi (Nyasaland), Malaysia (Malaya, Sarawak and N. Borneo), Singapore, Cyprus, Jamaica, Trinidad and Tobago have all become sovereign, independent members of the Commonwealth. South Africa has been obliged to leave the Commonwealth because of her determination to assert white supremacy over the African majority in her country. Egypt and the Sudan, Iraq and Jordan have become independent again and like Burma are not Commonwealth members.

The British Empire has passed into history, dissolved by the pressure of rising nationalism in countries which were previously administered as British colonies, whose populations now have educated leaders of their own, anxious to control their own destinies. That the white rulers were generally pushed out more rapidly than they wished to go–or considered wise–is undeniable, but perhaps nothing is more to our credit than that we nowhere bitterly fought to stay, everywhere left behind us viable and generally friendly new states, sometimes, especially in Africa, modern states created by our administration out of the many different tribes in an area defined originally by conquest and by the competing pressures of other European nations in the course of centuries of European wars and in the nineteenth century 'Scramble for Africa'.

Sometimes these new nations have difficulty in holding together–the strains shown by the Nigerian Federation bear witness to this. Sometimes our Westminster democracy, with one party in power and another in opposition has given way to dictatorship, as in Pakistan and Ghana. There are several forms of government in the new states, of which one of the most original is the single-party democracy of Tanzania, with real competition between candidates for Parliament. Several of the new nations (India, Pakistan, Ghana) are republics, but continue to accept the Queen as Head of the Commonwealth.

This Commonwealth which has replaced the Empire is now an association of equal white and coloured peoples, the first since the Roman Empire, if Rome is comparable, and unique in the modern world. Inevitably it faces the problems posed by its great differences of culture and level of culture, religion, history and language, as well as of climate and wealth. There are also immense differences in population, from India's 472 million, Pakistan's 107 million, Nigeria's nearly 56 million (roughly the same as the United Kingdom), to Canada's 19 million, Australia's 11 million, the 10 million each of Kenya, Tanzania and Malaysia, to the approximately 4 million each of Zambia and Malawi, the $2\frac{1}{2}$ million of New Zealand and the 827 thousand of Trinidad—each equally entitled to send the head of its government to the Commonwealth Prime Minister's Conference. In this association, held together by mutual desire and the ability by cohesion to further each other's interests, the coloured peoples now greatly outnumber the white.

Probably the Commonwealth's greatest difficulty lies in the great disparity in its members' standard of living. This varies—insofar as such international comparisons reduced to £ s. d. are valid—from Canada's yearly income per head of £570, Australia's £544, the approximate £450 of the United Kingdom and New Zealand, to (next in order and note the drop) Cyprus £193, Malta £140, Jamaica £132, Ghana £80, Malaysia (with Singapore) £53, Ceylon £43, Nigeria £35, India and Pakistan, with their immense populations, about £25 per head.[1] Many of these countries depend on 'primary products', exporting food and the raw materials of industry, with often violently fluctuating prices, and often too depend heavily on a single crop, such as cocoa. Some, such as Eastern Nigeria, have found oil, all are striving to create the industries by which they hope to climb out of poverty, although still basically agricultural countries. They seek aid from the advanced industrial countries of the world, which

[1] *Guardian*, 17.6.65.

Britain gives within her limited means and which is given generously in many forms by the U.S.A., partly (but only partly) to forestall Russian and Chinese aid and the influence which may go with it.

We have still to finish the story of the emancipation of China. After the fall of the Manchu emperors, Sun Yat-sen was elected President in 1912, but he died (an avowed supporter of Communism) in 1916 and the vast domain of China was split up between ambitious war-lords, each intent on furthering his own ambitions with his own private army. It was not until 1927 that Chiang Kai-shek was able to re-establish a central authority and he dismissed the Communist advisers who had been brought in from Russia. But within ten years his grasp was being loosened by the Japanese attacks and for twelve further years the patient Chinese peasant—in many places seldom more than a hand's breadth from famine in any case—was at the mercy of roving bandits, owing more or less allegiance to one or other war-lord, but pillaging and killing at will.

One of the private armies in the State was that of the Chinese Communist Party, founded—like our own Communist Party—in 1920. Unlike the British, the Chinese Communist Party met with considerable success, for it brought in the doctrines of the Soviet Revolution before the Chinese had been able to consolidate their own revolution, before their intellectual leaders had been able to think out new theories to replace or bring up to date the ancient ways of Confucianism. India achieved a religious revival, Japan copied the material successes of the West without losing her own clearly-defined social organisation and religion, Siam and Burma had their own vigorous faiths—not so China. Until 1945 the Chinese Communists fought alongside the Chiang Kai-shek Government against the Japanese invader; after the collapse of Japan the two Chinese factions fought each other. Both American mediation and American aid to Chiang Kai-shek were unsuccessful. He was defeated and withdrew to the island of Formosa with the remains of his army. The Communist People's Republic of China was established in October 1949.

It seemed at first that the industrialisation of China might be

Nuffield Organisation

11 Morris Motors Chassis Assembly Shop, Old Military College, Cowley, 1913.

12. "Music and entertainment will be with you wherever you drive, if you take along one of these portable 'super-hets'"—caption of the nineteen twenties.

Courtesy of the London County Council

13. The Social Revolution: groups from the same school photographed in 1894, 1924 and 1953.

undertaken by the U.S.S.R. but China has cast off Russian apron strings and the two are now rivals for the leadership of the Communist world, as well as for the support of the uncommitted nations. As the hostility between the U.S.S.R. and the West diminishes, so China, with its population of 640 millions,[1] some day to be armed with atomic weapons, becomes one of the dominant nations of the future. The international conference which met in Geneva in July 1954 to end the fighting in Indo-China was historic, for there, for the first time, the West was confronted by revolutionary Asia, represented by China, North Korea and North Vietnam, and speaking as an equal. The new Chinese Government–turning its back on the humiliations of the nineteenth century–asserted its position as one of the world's Great Powers. The underlying issue of that conference was the American effort to contain the explosive force of the Chinese revolution and the Chinese attempt to exclude the West altogether from Asia. Significantly in the balance between the two are the new states of emancipated Asia–freed from Western imperialism, not subject to Communist imperialism–namely India, Pakistan, Ceylon, Burma, Indonesia.

(iii)

'Triumph and Tragedy'–final volume of *The Second World War* by WINSTON S. CHURCHILL

When the Second World War ended the mutual distrust between the Communist U.S.S.R. and her Western allies–to have united them against him was one of Hitler's more remarkable achievements–came to the surface as each (but more particularly the Russians) occupied the most favourable accessible positions for what became the 'Cold War' between the Communists and the West. On Japan's surrender the U.S.A. occupied the southern part of Korea, long subject to the rivalry of China, Japan and Russia. The U.S.S.R. sent troops into northern Korea and, as in East Germany, set up a Communist government. When both American and Russian forces withdrew in 1950 the governments of North and South Korea went to war, the Communist north, with Russian tanks, quickly reaching the

---

[1] The population of Great Britain is 54 million.

southern capital, where however, they were halted by something new, a United Nations army, with soldiers from 16 nations, although predominantly American and under an American commander. After much bloodshed it drove the Communists back, capturing the northern capital and this again produced a new phenomenon, an army from resurgent Communist China. Painfully this too was defeated by the United Nations forces by mid 1951 and after two years of negotiations an armistice was signed in 1953. The two Koreas have faced each other across the armistice line ever since.

President Roosevelt died on 12th April 1945 at the supreme climax of the statesman's war and at the juncture when his authority and experience were most needed. He was succeeded by his Vice-President, Harry S. Truman. The American Vice-President is an understudy, with no active role of any importance. Not widely known, he watches the brilliant performance of his principal from the dress-circle. That Mr. Truman–who formally authorised the dropping of the two atomic bombs and put American troops into Korea before Congress had given its view–proved to be a man equal to his crushing responsibilities we now know, but it was unfortunate that the understudy should be called just when the performance needed to be changed.

Mr. Churchill had urged–without success–that the Anglo-American forces should be allowed to strike northwards from Italy into the Balkans and liberate part of Central Europe. On 30th April 1945 he begged, again unsuccessfully, that at least Prague might be liberated by General Eisenhower's advancing armies, but the Americans were determined to abide by pre-conceived military plans and declined to raise their eyes to the wide political horizon. A few days later Mr. Churchill cabled to Mr. Eden, then in San Francisco: '. . . The proposed withdrawal of the United States Army to the occupational lines which were arranged with the Russians and Americans in Quebec, and which were marked in yellow on the maps we studied there, would mean the tide of Russian domination sweeping forward 120 miles on a front of 300 or 400 miles. . . . After it was over and the territory occupied by the Russians Poland[1] would be completely

[1] For whom we went to war.

engulfed and buried deep in Russian lands . . . the territories under Russian control would include the Baltic provinces, all of Germany to the occupational line, all Czechoslovakia, a large part of Austria, the whole of Yugoslavia, Hungary, Roumania, Bulgaria, until Greece in her present tottering condition is reached. It would include all the great capitals of Middle Europe, including Berlin, Vienna, Budapest, Belgrade, Bucharest, and Sofia. . . . This constitutes an event in the history of Europe to which there has been no parallel, and which has not been faced by the Allies in their long and hazardous struggle.'[1] (Militarily and economically these countries, apart from Yugoslavia and Austria, are now integrated with the U.S.S.R.). On 12th May 1945 he cabled to Mr. Truman: '. . . An iron curtain is drawn down upon their front. We do not know what is going on behind.'

The lines defining the areas to be occupied by the different Allies and marked in yellow on the map to which Mr. Churchill referred were those drawn in 1943 by a committee consisting of the Soviet and American Ambassadors, Mr. Gusev and Mr. Winant, and Sir William Strang of the Foreign Office. They were made available, as a matter of convenience, to the commanders in the field, in anticipation of the time when Germany should be overrun by the Allies, but in 1943–before the Normandy landings–that time seemed remote and uncertain and the committee's proposals were pigeonholed. It is interesting to contrast the amount of thought given to the drawing of those yellow lines with the research, discussion and trouble taken over the adjustment of frontiers in 1919–20, for without further discussion the yellow lines have become the boundary between the Communist and the Western worlds.

The 'Cold War' between Communism and the West was really an arms race between the U.S.A. and the U.S.S.R.–Great Britain, although technically qualified, being unable to maintain the terrific rate of spending involved. It seems to have stabilised in a balance of horror, each of these two super Powers standing by able and ready at any instant day and night to destroy the majority of each other's cities and population, and probably much

[1] *Triumph and Tragedy* (Cassell, 1954).

of the rest of the race at the same time.[1] A climax was reached when the small island of Cuba, just south of the United States, went Communist in 1962 and the U.S.S.R. installed rocket sites there from which nuclear missiles could have hit the U.S.A. with virtually no warning. There was a week of tension while President Kennedy and Mr. Khrushchev tested each other's nerve before the Russians sensibly withdrew from their exposed position on the far side of the Atlantic. Russia becoming more 'comfortable' is to-day also closer to the West in outlook and preoccupied with her vast and now unfriendly neighbour China.

Our last section described the receding tide of empire, the end of the long period in which Europe and Europe's wars dominated world affairs. It described particularly how the British colonies became independent, but the same is true of the French, Dutch and Belgian colonies. Now throughout Africa there are sovereign states and the African governs himself, except in South Africa, the Portuguese colonies and Rhodesia. In these area white minorities in a black continent dominate seas of black Africans who threaten at any moment to engulf them violently, unless they cede government to the majority as wisely as did the white Kenyans—of which there is as yet no sign.

The ebb of empire has increased by dozens the number of new nations—in 1960 alone there were sixteen new nations. Each has its vote in the United Nations Assembly. Although the great Powers still dominate—without China which unwisely has never been admitted to U.N.O.—the combined votes of these new nations can often defeat the manipulations of the Powers. The United States, which could count on the support of the states of South America, must now also woo those of Africa.

Nearly all these new nations have in common their poverty. In Western countries the infant at birth can look forward—if he thinks to do so—to a life of nearly seventy years (still only the Biblical three score and ten), but for the great majority of the

---

[1] 'There is an immense gulf between the atomic and the hydrogen bomb. The atomic bomb, with all its terrors, did not carry us outside the scope of human control or manageable events, in thought or action, in peace or war. When the chairman of the United States Congressional Committee gave out, a year ago, the first comprehensive review of the hydrogen bomb, the entire foundation of human affairs was revolutionised, and mankind placed in a situation both measureless and laden with doom'—Sir Winston Churchill in the House of Commons, 1st March 1955.

world's children the average span of life is still only about thirty years. In most of the cities of Africa and Asia the ordinary worker's home is a single room, with a share of cooking, washing and toilet facilities. If that, for those who have travelled there will often have seen a family living at the roadside, the mother squatting over some nameless stew in a pot on a heap of sticks, the children crouched on their small bundles of possessions –the only home they know. And the poor peoples are mostly the non-white peoples, for the division between riches and poverty runs dangerously along the line between white and coloured in the world's population. '. . . the average real income of the 200 million people of North America is nearly 25 times as high as that of the over 1,600 million people of Asia'.[1]

The world's population continues to grow, not because the birth-rate rises but because modern medicine and sanitation bring down the death-rate, sometimes sensationally, as when malaria is eliminated from a whole area. It is the population of the poorer countries–of the Indian subcontinent, South America and Asia–which grows most rapidly. All India's heroic efforts, within the framework of a real democracy, to achieve economic development comparable to that enforced by the Communist Party on the Russian people, all the help given her by the West, have done no more than provide her increasing total of inhabitants with the barest, inadequate ration. In China, the population increases by 12 million–twice the total population of England in 1700–every year. 'In A.D. 1600 the total number of people in the world was only about half a billion. It first reached one billion at about the end of the nineteenth century. By 1950 it had passed 2 billion. To-day it is $2\frac{3}{4}$ billion and increasing by nearly 50 million a year'.[2] This rising tide of humans presses dangerously on the ultimate value by which civilisation is judged, its respect for the individual human life.

[1] Sir Julian Huxley in the symposium *Our Crowded Planet*, edited by Fairfield Osborn (Allen & Unwin, 1963).

[2] Sir Julian Huxley op. cit. (written in 1962). In 1964 the world's population was estimated at about 3·2 billion (3,200 million). The Commonwealth embraces about one quarter of the total, Communist states one third.

9

Changing Ways of Life

Since 1900

DESPITE war, revolution, crisis and startling scientific advance babies have still to be washed, meals cooked and beds made. It is indeed a tribute to the mental toughness of human beings that after each of the cataclysms of our time we have settled down again as well as possible to the ordinary affairs of life. But technical and social change have radically affected the framework within which we carry out the eternal functions of eating and washing-up, work and sleep.

We seek the lady of the house as she was any time before about 1920. Is she in her bedroom? Note the iron bedstead, with its high iron rails at head and foot, surmounted by four brass knobs at the corners. Against the wall is a marble-topped washstand, carrying a china basin in which stands a big jug of cold water—on the right a small glass water-bottle for cleaning the teeth, always kept with an inverted tumbler over its neck. Is she perhaps in her kitchen? We notice the knife-board, for stainless steel was not invented until 1913 and cleaning the knives with paste is still a weekly routine. There is also no convenient detergent to squeeze out of a plastic container, only the old sand-soap to cope with grease. Against one wall is a row of cow-bells hanging on springs. When the visitor at the door or the lady of the house in the remote upper quarters wants attention she pulls at one end of a long wire whose farther end budges just sufficiently to set the appropriate bell jangling. If it is summer you may be shocked by the buzzing of flies and bluebottles. But then most of the traffic outside is still horsedrawn; cartloads of horse-droppings

are taken off the streets every day, and where there is dung
there are flies. The dustcarts incidentally are still open farm carts;
when it is windy their lighter contents are apt to be whirled up
into the air.

The milkman comes round on a light milk-float, standing on the
step at the back, the big milk-churn in front of him balanced
over the wheels. You hear the clip-clop of the horse's neatly
shod feet coming down the road of a morning and the cheerful
yodel 'Milk-o' brings the maid to the back door with her jugs,
into which the milk is ladled from a pail. At tea-time you may
still hear the muffin-man come round with his bell, held stiffly
outstretched as he maintains the balance of the covered tray on
his head. The grocer's is a place of romance, with the friendly
hiss of the lights as they throw sharp shadows against the dark
walls, the shelves right up to the ceiling behind the long counter,
the boxes of tea, sugar, flour and rice, the barrels of butter and
casks of lard out of which the grocer weighs your portion, for
these goods do not yet arrive already weighed, wrapped and
branded with their maker's name, and the phrase 'untouched by
hand' has yet to be invented. The intriguing smell is probably
a mixture of ginger, coffee, cinnamon, tea, cheese, soap, oil and
mice. Tea the grocer may blend himself, measuring out the
quantities on to a piece of paper on the counter, which he then
expertly twists up into a packet. The jam arrives chiefly in
earthenware pots, but tinned Californian fruit was an early
arrival and by the end of the First War there are other tinned
goods: soup, salmon, corned beef and potted meat in jars. Perhaps we should just remind you that all the work in the home is
done by hand; the day of household machinery has not yet
dawned.

Here at last is the lady of the house herself. And the first thing
we notice about her is that her face is as nature made it. Cosmetics
were known to the most ancient civilisations of which we have
record, but for eighty years down to 1918 they were the mark
of the harlot. The nineteen-twenties saw the introduction of lip-
stick, eyebrow and eyelash colouring, but at first only on the
stage. The respectable lady of the house certainly did not use
such things and her husband would have been most distressed to

have found them on her dressing-table. Later on society began to imitate the actress; cosmetics gradually spread to the working girl and ultimately to the suburban housewife. But certainly not until the nineteen-thirties would she be seen applying them in public, and at the beginning of the century only a very head-strong woman would smoke a cigarette. No industry, except per-haps tobacco, has gained as much as have cosmetics from the emancipation of women.[1]

The clothes worn by the lady of the house at the beginning of our period are familiar enough from her picture. The skirt came down to the ground and contained as much cloth as went into a complete long-sleeved dress after the war. The bustle had already gone out, but beneath the skirt there were still one or more petticoats and a formidably stiff corset. 'The master's' clothes were equally formal, for at the beginning of the century the square-cut frock-coat was still the only correct garment for the middle and upper classes except in the country or for sport. The morning-coat appeared soon after, but was still necessarily crowned by a top-hat. The bowler remained the sign of the superior artisan, and below this social level the workman wore a cloth cap, often copied by his wife, who skewered it on with an enormous hatpin. Our generation is accustomed to seeing men in uniform and to reading off a good deal of information about an individual's formation, unit and past experience from the coloured 'flashes' on his sleeve and the medal ribbons on his breast. The sharp class distinctions of that past age could be read off even more clearly in the different clothes, so that you knew at once to what manner of man or woman you were speak-ing. Even the heavy boots of the labourer were distinct from the neatly buttoned boots of the professional man—probably protected by rubber goloshes in wet weather. All classes gloried in quan-tities of buttons, hooks-and-eyes and snappers, although zip-fasteners began to come into use between the wars.

---

[1] Today the cost of the actual materials may be only one-quarter of the cost of the romantic containers into which they are put. '. . . even the best of the preparations might on analysis seem disappointingly prosaic to those who are accustomed to think in terms of petal bloom and breathtaking loveliness. A typical face powder is talc, kaolin, mag-nesium stearate and zinc oxide. Cold cream is usually water emulsified with, say, borax and beeswax, in mineral oil'—*Economist*, April 1954.

For the lady of the house a ride in a motor-car was quite an experience, but early in the century the 'safety bicycle', which was already substantially the bicycle as we know it, had become familiar even to the humbler middle-class families. It gave its possessor a personal mobility which had previously been enjoyed only by the rider and the carriage-owner. The bicycle conferred the freedom of the open road, and before 1914 the roads were indeed open, unencumbered and inviting.

By 1914 London had about one hundred picture palaces, but few had been specially built on the grand scale to which we are accustomed. One of the first was the New Gallery in Regent Street which was opened in 1913. The silent film was accompanied by a small orchestra or single pianist, who endeavoured to keep up a constant flow of music more or less appropriate to the action being shown on the somewhat flickering screen, and incidentally managed to drown the clicking of the early projector. Writing in 1923, an authority reports: 'During the last few years the demand for the picture play has enabled each film company to maintain in regular employment a company of actors and actresses.'

BETWEEN THE WARS

After the war women got the vote without further argument, in two stages: those over 30 in 1918 and the young things between 21 and 30 in 1928. The Representation of the People Act of 1918 increased the number of voters from 8 to about 18 million, of whom rather less than half were women. They were making their presence increasingly apparent in the professions, in business and in factories. Indeed as one marriageable man in seven had been killed in the war and another seriously injured, it is not surprising that after it was over women clung to such jobs as the trade unions would let them hold. At the same time also the woman of the privileged classes stepped out of the cocoon in which Victorian and Edwardian convention had enwrapped her. Gone were the chaperones, gone the days when she walked out (except in 'safe' areas) escorted by her maid; gone also the afternoons spent in a leisurely way with Mamma, driving round to pay social calls or to leave pasteboard visiting cards. Some part of this social intercourse would now be carried out by telephone, less graciously but with a great saving of time, and leisure was one of the casualties of war. No longer was the young lady of this class brought up to know with effortless ease how to address the younger son of an earl or his dowager mother, to know the relationship of all the best families and to regard as very doubtful the social status of those engaged in trade. No longer was her life almost wholly preoccupied with the social round and its intricate convention. After the Second World War the daughters of these sheltered Edwardian girls would retain hardly a trace of what their mothers had been. They would be women with careers, secretaries, 'ex-service personnel'. As Mrs. Olive Heseltine put it in that poignant memoir of her youth which she called *Lost Content*: 'And although towards the end of the century the high noon of Victorian greatness was past, sunshine still glowed on its hour of afternoon tea. . . . Not for a moment could they have dreamed that their civilisation, so slowly and painfully elaborated, so orderly, respectable and enlightened, would twice be mortally assailed; that their grand-daughters, slumbering peacefully in their perambulators, would find themselves maids of all work in unheated houses, cooking, sweeping, scrubbing, minding babies, tending sick-beds, standing eternally in queues; whilst their grandsons, who had faced death in African deserts, Asiatic jungles and Arctic seas, discharged from hospitals, from mental homes, from German prison camps, returned at last to help wash dishes, black the boots and carry up the coals. . . .'[1]

The loss of leisure and the growing scarcity of servants called for the simplification of social life in every way and as middle-class women found themselves doing their own housework they set up a demand for more labour-saving household appliances. There entered the household scene such things as soap-flakes, preparations like Vim, Mirro, etc.; coffee was bought already ground; and with the growing use of motor vehicles the larger shops were willing to deliver goods at the door. It became possible to order by telephone, and this was made easier by the increasing standardisation of goods, brought about by mass

1 Privately printed, 1948.

production. Woolworth's first branch had been opened in Liverpool in 1906 and Marks and Spencer's Penny Bazaars were a familiar institution before 1914, but these and other chain stores spread rapidly after 1918. It became quite common to take the main midday meal in a restaurant. Apart from pubs and the chop-house providing a solid meal for solid men, before the First War restaurants were rather a luxurious rarity, designed to add to the exotic pleasures of the rich. The mass feeding establish-ments which we take for granted in large towns only developed rapidly after the war. Vitamins A, B and C were familiar in the nineteen-twenties, which also saw the arrival of those intricate ice-creams whose glamorous names like Knickerbocker Glory reveal their American origin.

Hair was often bobbed after the war. Skirts similarly retreated to about knee-level, and have remained not much below the knee ever since. Clothing became altogether simpler. The lady of the house whom we visited before the war was wearing clothes which could be weighed in pounds. The weight of her daughter's clothes ten or fifteen years later was a matter of ounces. Her daughter's young husband wore a lounge suit for practically all purposes and, unlike his father, he sported no monocle, cane, tie-pin or spats. Both husband and wife would don gaily-coloured pullovers at week-ends—the beginning of the tendency for men's and women's sporting clothes to become similar, largely through the female copying the male. But unquestionably the most important develop-ment lay in the fact that for the first time in history a large amount of clothing was woven from a fibre found in neither plant nor animal world but manufactured from cellulose by man. British yearly output of artificial silk or 'rayon' had been a matter of 200,000 lbs. in the years 1907–9; by 1919 it was 35 million, and in the following decade it increased tenfold.

The great quickening in the pace of scientific advance and of man's mastery over matter had its effect on entertainment and instruction, which could now be carried out by the intangible medium of wireless. The thermionic valve, the essential com-ponent in modern wireless and sound amplification, had been invented by Professor J. A. Fleming at the turn of the century. In 1922 a monopoly of broadcasting was given to the British

Broadcasting Company, whose principal shareholders were the six largest manufacturers of wireless equipment. In December of that year the weekly programme consisted of 23½ hours of music, 3 hours news, 1 hour religion, 5¼ hours for children and ¾ hour of talks. Dance music, variety and drama were added to the programme in 1923. By 1926 the success of the venture was apparent and the company was bought out by a public corporation, the British Broadcasting Corporation. By the end of 1930 there were already nearly 2 million holders of wireless licences, and on 2nd November 1936 the B.B.C. started to broadcast a daily two-hours programme of television. Nineteen twenty-seven had already seen the arrival of sound films, with their own incidental music, now often specially composed. By 1934 weekly cinema attendances in Great Britain probably totalled something like 18½ million, and by 1945 this figure had grown to 30 million. Within a single generation two inventions had established themselves and become institutions which are now as much part of our lives as the weather, although the cinema has declined as a result of TV.

The internal combustion engine is the other invention which has changed our whole way of living within a single lifetime. The development of motor-car, coach, lorry and aeroplane was probably more important than anything else that happened in the period, except the entry of women into public life. It was in the first two or three years after the war that it became usual for a middle-class family to own a car, and between 1919 and 1921 the number of cars licensed multiplied fivefold–from 50,000 to 250,000. Three years later Austin made the first serious attempt in this country to produce a car within the means of a really large number of purses; the famous Austin Seven was offered at £165. It was in the nineteen-twenties that buses began to appear with covered tops, so that it was no longer necessary for those on top to rely on a mackintosh apron with which to cover their laps when it rained (hooked on to the back of the seat at either end), and smokers were no longer exhorted to sit at the back. Charabancs too developed from the early car with benches into something approaching the modern coach, and with the improvements in the vehicle went its greatly extended use, at first only for excursions, but in the 'thirties as a competitor to the railways. Buses tended to replace trams; local bus services linked village with village and village with town, so that the people from over the horizon were no longer strangers. Or ought one to say that we all became superficially acquainted and basically strangers, for the new mobility broke up the deep intimacy of isolated communities; people began to up sticks and change their dwelling-place more often; local news faded before B.B.C. news, as did also local accents.

Mobility and better communications naturally made for uniformity and the amalgamation of businesses into ever larger units of control. Until 1923 there was still a picturesque assortment of railway companies, each painting its rolling stock in its own distinctive 'livery', each with a staff which felt a jealous loyalty for the line, akin to that of a sailor for his ship or a soldier for his regiment. In 1923 four companies were formed out of the Great Western Railway, the Great Northern, Great Eastern, Great Central, London and North Western, London and South Western, the London, Brighton and South Coast, the Midland, North Eastern, North British, Great North of Scotland, Cambrian, Somerset and Dorset, etc. In 1948 the four companies became British Railways. Savings doubtless were achieved, but romance and rich variety were lost. The earlier companies can be traced to-day only on old notices or by inscriptions on bridges where their cast-iron signatures have not yet been effaced. Before 1918 the Big Five banks had already, by a series of amalgamations, grown to dominate their world, and between the wars Imperial Chemical Industries by the same process developed into a giant with a great preponderance in the country's heavy chemical industry. The London Passenger Transport Board obtained a complete monopoly of all sorts of transport in London, and after 1932 there was no place for the colourful but erratic 'pirate buses' which had dared to challenge the London General Omnibus Company's red-coated battalions—and had given Londoners an occasional thrill by swooping in ahead of an L.G.O.C. bus at a crowded stop.

But we have paid very dearly for the triumph of the internal combustion engine. About 1855 *The Times* printed a leading article on the danger of the roads, pointing out that in twelve months more than fifty people had been killed or run over in carriage accidents. In 1955 one hundred times as many were killed and 262,396 injured. On 17th August 1896, Mrs. Bridget Driscoll, a forty-four-year-old Irishwoman, was knocked down and killed by a private car travelling 'at the speed of a horse' –the first fatal accident involving a car. Between 1918 and 1939 some 120,000 people were similarly killed–a loss approximately equivalent to the strength of the original British Expeditionary Force; and some 1½ million people were also wounded on the roads. There were about 300,000 motor vehicles registered in 1913. Twenty-five years later, on the eve of the Second War, the number had increased tenfold and in 1964 was twelve million, at which point congestion in the great cities has almost brought the panting hordes to a standstill. Major Stanley, as Minister of Transport, introduced roundabouts, 'Major Road Ahead' signs and one-way streets; his successor, Mr. Hore-Belisha, brought in 'Belisha' or pedestrian crossings in 1934 and a speed limit of 30 m.p.h. in built-up areas. These devices have become familiar– a stream of their successors still seeks to keep traffic moving and to reduce the casualties. And some indication of what is involved can be gained by reflecting that there are now more than sixty vehicles for every mile of road, or more than one every 29 yards.

The car in the garage also tended to replace the child in the cot, or at any rate the second and third child, for few young couples could afford both, and between the wars many seem to have chosen the car. In 1911 the Census suggested that nearly half the families in the country had three or more children; by 1939 in was only a quarter who had that number. The average nine-teenth-century mother gave birth to five children, while between the wars the average was two children. But compared with the beginning of the century we now live about 20 years longer. In 1901 32 per cent of the population was under 15 and only 5 per cent over 64 years old; by 1953 only 22 per cent were under 15 and 11 per cent over 64. This is a result of both declining birth-rate and longer life. During the Great Depression in 1930 the birth-rate was only half that of 1871 and it seemed likely that the population would fall, but during the Second War there was an increase, and the population is now increasing again. (789,000 people were born in the U.K. in 1955; 1,012,900 in 1964). The threat of the atom bomb or of bacterial warfare seems less of a deterrent than the fear of unemployment. But anxiety and mobility–what is called the pace of modern life–make people irritable and contribute to divorce: mobility has spread to marriage. Before 1914 less than one-half of 1 per cent of marriages ended in divorce–a reflection in part of the subordinate position of women and of their difficulty in supporting themselves. Between the wars the proportion rose to 1·75 per cent. In 1938 the number of divorces granted was 6,092; by 1963 it had risen to 31,405.

We now live rather longer and retain our vigour to a more advanced age and this is due to better sanitation, a better understanding of nutrition and the great advance in medicine. To assess this you have only to consider the situation last century, before Lister's technique made it relatively safe for surgeons to open the abdominal cavity. A septic appendix is nowadays removed by an operation lasting only a few minutes and the patient is up and about again in ten days. Then it 'commonly led to an abscess which burst internally and caused death from peritonitis in a few hours or days'.[1] The triumphant advance of the chemical industry has provided a truly formidable array of preparations ranging from the vaccines prepared from anti-toxins produced in the animal body to synthetic drugs like paludrin or the sulphanilamides, to a mould like penicillin, to hormones replacing the functions of our own glands. Again, a vast array of chemico-physical appliances–X-rays, electron-microscopes, electro-cardiograms, isotopes–enables the specialist to find out what is going on inside the body to an extent which would dumbfound the earlier practitioner, who had to rely largely on sharp observation of external clinical signs interpreted in the light of his experience. The transfusion of fresh blood into a body from which life has almost ebbed has an effect which is miraculous almost in the same sense as the raising of Lazarus from the dead. And if mental diseases are only beginning to yield to these material

[1] F. Sherwood Taylor, *The Century of Science* (Heinemann, 1941).

methods, at least we are fully conversant with such psycho-analytical concepts as inferiority complexes, sadism, and the necessity of removing our inhibitions! All of these, together with the word 'relativity', have been common terms since the nineteen-twenties.

But let us return to our young couple with their single child in the last ten years before the Second World War. The first thing we notice is the still greater variety of their diet, for by then almost every kind of fruit and vegetable, home-grown or tropical, meat, game and fish could be got out of a tin. British production of tinned or bottled fruit and vegetables, like the British output of rayon, increased tenfold between the early 'twenties and the early 'thirties. Eating habits had changed, for in the thirty years after 1909 we doubled our average consumption of fruit and vegetables (other than potatoes), of butter, eggs and cheese. The consumption of milk increased substantially, that of white flour fell off. There were many more branded articles, often using cellophane or aluminium wrapping foil. The new lady of the house could fall back on ready-to-eat breakfast cereals instead of porridge, but cooking was made much easier for her than for her mother—or her mother's cook—by reason of the enterprising way in which half the work was done for her in the factories. Where her mother had anxiously collected recipes, lists and quantities of ingredients, she often merely added hot water or hot milk and, behold, the ingredients cunningly concentrated in the packet blossomed, swelled in her dish and became custard, blancmange, or jelly, while self-raising flour performed its miracle infallibly.

Yet in some ways the most remarkable thing about our young family is the difficulty in singling it out, for clothes are now largely made by machine and those worn by all classes look much the same. (True, the young man still has his suits cut by hand by his own tailor—but the difference between the result, pleasing as it is, and that achieved by the Fifty Shilling Tailors is not the difference between his father's morning-coat and the gardener's corduroys.) Indeed, as Mr. Muggeridge put it characteristically at the time: 'There has been a general toning-down process, an endeavour, which tends to become desperate, to soften the asperities of social and economic inequality by pretending they scarcely exist. . . . Wealth, which used to be respected, has come merely to be envied; and the well-to-do find it necessary either to be apologetic or to become socialists.'[1] The Colonel's lady and Judy O'Grady were already sisters who dressed alike.

Between 1913 and 1937 the employed worker increased his outlay on clothes by about half, but he spent two and a quarter times as much on his home. By 1939 most middle-class families were in dwellings built after 1920, while working-class families still generally occupied nineteenth-century buildings–often the big houses left vacant by Victorian and Edwardian families, now awkwardly cut up into flats and maisonettes. The evils which Jack London described were largely overcome by a vigorous effort to reduce overcrowding and–particularly after 1933–to clear away verminous, worn-out slums. By 1939 gross overcrowding was past, except in the East End of London, on Tyneside and in Scotland. (Yet even in 1937 in eighteen metropolitan boroughs north of the Thames only 10 per cent of working-class families claimed so much as a share in a bathroom.) After 1918 living in flats became more common, and the better newly-built flats boasted central heating. But most couples still wanted their own little house, and wanted it as different as possible from the house of anybody else, and it is these 'long, spindly fingers of villas' which stretched ever farther along the main roads into what had been the country. Forty per cent of the British people lived in London, Manchester, Birmingham, West Yorkshire, Glasgow, Merseyside and Tyneside. In the period between the wars the suburbs of these seven 'conurbations' expanded by 32 per cent; almost two-thirds of the national increase in dwellings over eighteen years went into them, particularly into the suburbs of the relatively prosperous southern and midland clots of humanity.[2]

The new lower-middle class was bound together by the unfamiliar worries and aspirations of this new suburban world: 'putting aside enough to meet the payments to the building

[1] *The Thirties.* It was just before the Second World War that 'nylon' joined 'rayon' as the second of the artificial fabrics.

[2] After the Second World War there was a bitter shortage of dwellings because many had been destroyed; there were more separate families (owing to the higher proportion of adults in the population), and rent restriction hampered movement. It caused people to take more space than they would otherwise have done, because their old, large house might be cheaper than a new, small one. But there was no return to overcrowding.

K

society, to maintain enough insurance to protect the widow and the children . . outside the State insurance schemes, to buy a three-monthly season ticket for the journey between home and office, to pay secondary school fees for sons and daughters who must not take up manual labour, and to cover the doctors' fees for those "not on the panel"; not the least of the changes were those that hovered between the field of social obligation and relaxation–the cost of keeping the flower-beds well tended, of keeping the small week-end car in good repair and of rebuilding the savings depleted by the summer holiday.'[1]

Holidays without loss of pay began to become much more general just before the Second War broke out, and in 1938 11½ million workers had this privilege, previously restricted to clerks and foremen. Since 1945 it has become general, with the result that the golden sands, once the preserve of the few, are now almost as crowded in August as the great cities during the rest of the year. Some towns, such as Blackpool, Margate and Southend, were early in the commercialisation of the sea-front in order to entertain and exploit these big crowds, just as Brighton had long before set out to cater for their privileged predecessors. In 1935 Mr. Butlin started his first holiday camp in Skegness. After his second camp was opened in Clacton he was able to report that 250,000 people visited the two camps in a year and between them spent only just under £1 million on the recreations and services he offered. But between the wars foreign travel also ceased to be the monopoly of the wealthy and even the humblest slipped across to the French and Belgian Channel resorts, where they got that first-hand 'feel' of a foreign country which so many of the younger generation were soon to get almost to excess and in all parts of the world at the invitation of the armed forces. In the 'thirties during the Great Depression the shipping companies sought to recoup themselves for the loss of American tourist traffic by offering cruises–at middle-class rates and in their holiday periods–to such delectable places as Morocco, the Canaries, Spain and Portugal, Norway or the Western Mediterranean. Nor did they neglect to provide dances on board, swimming, fancy-dress parties, concerts and deck-games.

[1] M. Abrams, *Condition of the British People, 1911–45* (Gollancz, 1946).

About the same time hiking became very popular and youth hostels spread beneficently across the countryside. There was a movement to get into the country for recreation, and it is interesting that most of the younger generation between the wars learned to swim. Before 1914 few of the poorer children had the opportunity, unless they lived on the coast, but now swimming-baths were provided by the municipalities and visited by school-children with their teachers. Drunkenness and street fighting continued to decline; since about 1930 people have on the whole been drinking half as much as in 1900 but smoking two and a half times as much. Amateur football teams sprang up all over the country when the men returned after the First War and began the weekly matches between towns, villages and works teams which we take for granted to-day as part of the social scene. But it was not long before football became commercialised. Soccer has developed into an industry, with astute managements investing shrewdly in good players of the sort who can be relied upon to draw immense audiences, with correspondingly large box-office receipts, and who can also be 'sold' to another club for a fee running into thousands of pounds. The professional players have their own trade union. Football pools were initiated in the 'thirties. Dog-racing started in Manchester in July 1926, and in the following year sixty-two greyhound racing tracks were registered in Great Britain. Watching professional football, filling in the Pools forms, Bingo and betting are our national pastimes.

They are all pastimes which depend on mobility and good communications, on the ability of large crowds to collect and disperse quickly, on newspapers and wireless which whip up enthusiasm and later announce the winners, on the ubiquitous postal services without which the Pools would cease to exist. The same good communications are used by the public relations officer. He came into being between the wars and his task is by all means in his power to influence public opinion in favour of the organisation–or individual–by which he is employed, to defend it if attacked; to *explain* it to the public. That the methods of the public relations officer can be abused for the purposes of propaganda we need hardly remind a generation which has lived within sound of Hitler and Mussolini–and by propaganda we mean the deliberate attempt to heat up the emotions so that they fuse the brain. Shortly after this new profession of influencing opinion first became established Mr. Muggeridge wrote: 'Publicity became a mighty industry, whose annual turnover ran into millions, whose captains were knighted and in other ways honoured, a cult, almost a religion, with many devotees. Actresses, politicians, athletes, authors had their publicity agents, whose business was to make their light shine before men, and keep it shining. Government departments and business enterprises required public relations officers, for the same purpose.'[1] It has indeed been called 'an age of sensational and mendacious advertisement, an age in which good salesmanship sells more than good workmanship'.[2]

TECHNICAL CHANGE

The emancipation of women, mobility, social uniformity, wireless, films, motor-cars—these have been the main factors in our changing way of living. It remains to describe further effects of violent scientific and technical advance, and we start with electricity, which has become our ubiquitous servant in the last fifty years. '. . . at the end of the 'eighties the industry was still (if we exclude the . . . Ferranti station at Deptford) represented by a number of small corrugated-iron huts clustered around the Metropolitan area and dotted sparsely about the provinces, fitted with clanking machinery which supplied a few hundred lamps within a radius of not much more than half a mile of the "station".'[3] In the 'twenties we had the first electric kettles (with their heating elements in the lid) and the first electrically heated irons for laundries.

In the 'thirties the beneficent small electric motor began to enter a large number of homes inside the vacuum cleaner, which is now increasingly often accompanied by the washing-machine, the hair-dryer, the refrigerator, the cake-mixer, the electric razor and the electric sewing-machine. In industry at the turn of the century most workshops were still equipped with long lines of overhead shafting from which the machines below were driven by belts and pulleys: above a mass of whirling wheels, with drip

---

[1] *The Thirties.*   [2] Somervell, *op. cit.*   [3] *Financial News,* 25th March 1935.

cans to catch the oil from the bearings, and leading down from them a restless forest of belting. Moreover, it is not easy to make power from a shaft go round a bend and the hampering effect of this arrangement on factory layout may be imagined. From all this, industry was freed after the First War by equipping each machine with its own electric motor, to be switched on or off irrespective of the rest. It enabled the machine to be placed anywhere in the factory and the factory is no longer obliged to hug the railway, because its power comes by electric cable and its materials and products, unless they are very heavy, can be moved by lorry. Another great advantage was found in the general adoption of ball-bearings, which made it possible for machinery on the whole to become much lighter and of course reduced friction to a miraculous extent. No less miraculous would oxy-acetylene welding and cutting have seemed to the Edwardian workman who was obliged to saw or chisel through steel.

Dr. Rudolph Diesel first showed his oil engine in 1900. Three years later he showed one of 80 h.p., and by 1908 there were diesels of 1,000 h.p. 'It was stated in *Cassier's Magazine* (of 1911) that if Diesel engines of 1,500 horse-power per cylinder were installed in the *Mauretania* the 70,000 horse power of that vessel could be produced in one-fifth of the space occupied by the boilers and turbines. The need for coal trimming and stoking would be abolished; it would be possible to dispense with 192 stokers and 120 trimmers. . . .'[1] This dream has since been realised, although the large modern liner is now powered by oil-fired steam turbines instead of marine diesels. Some notion of the complexity and interdependence of modern industry can perhaps be grasped from this list of the materials used in the 'twenties in an ordinary electric lamp: tungsten, tin, lead, nickel, copper, iron, zinc, glass (consisting of sand, soda, nitre, manganese, arsenic, litharge, feldspar, lime, lead, cobalt, potash) and basing cement (consisting in turn of alcohol, marble dust, pine resin, shellac chalk, bakelite, glyptal and malachite green). Or an idea of the importance of science in the daily routine can be gleaned from the glimpse of one large firm of caterers starting

[1] Edward Cressy, *Discoveries and Inventions of the Twentieth Century* (Routledge, 2nd edn., 1923).

in 1918 to employ one chemist, with one assistant and a typist, and twenty years later finding that its research staff of 200 were carrying out 85,000 routine examinations a year. Now a giant organisation such as the Shell Petroleum Co. employs nearly 5,000 scientists.

The most important of the new materials was obviously aluminium, of which world production was 283 lbs. in 1885, 8,000 tons in 1902, about 750,000 in 1939 and about 3 million tons in 1943, followed by plastics, of which the first, bakelite, was discovered by Baekeland in 1906. By 1939 half a million British workers were employed in manufacturing plastics and— somewhat to the dismay of those who regret the passing of brass— they have become a standard material for electric fittings, ash-trays, fountain-pens, bathroom fittings, cupboard handles, lava-tory seats and aeroplane parts. The rise of new industries in the 'twenties and 'thirties is graphically shown (to readers with no abhorrence of figures) by the fact that those employed in elec-trical wiring and contracting increased more than threefold (321 per cent) between 1923 and 1936, the number of those in rayon manufacture more than doubled, and those making motors, cycles and aircraft increased by 60 per cent.

The Wright brothers first made a flight of twenty-four miles in 1905. By 1919 Captain Alcock and Lieutenant Brown of the R.A.F. were able to fly over 2,000 miles across the Atlantic—such was the impetuous speed with which man's age-old dream of flight was realised once the principles of aerodynamics were established and the internal-combustion engine could give a re-latively light source of sufficient power. In August 1919 the first daily air service for passengers and goods in the world was opened between Hounslow, just outside London, and Paris. 'I remember quite clearly,' wrote Mr. Harper,[1] 'seeing a couple of passengers, resigned but still apprehensive, being packed into one of these small aeroplanes like sardines in a tin. There seemed barely room for them to sit in the tiny cabin facing each other. And then when they had been tucked into their places and seemed in-capable of doing more than move their heads slightly, a sort of metal lid was shut down with a clang and fastened into position

[1] *The Romance of a Modern Airway*, quoted Cressy, *op. cit.*

above their heads.' We can get an idea of these early planes from Mr. Cressy's account in 1923: 'The monoplane constructed by Messrs. Vickers Ltd. . . . has a frame of weldless steel tubes which carries the fuselage and wings. The rudder is actuated by a foot-bar, and a universal lever enables the wings to be warped and the elevator to be raised or lowered. The wings are made of ash, and are covered with an extremely strong light material with a smooth surface which is impervious to water. All metal parts are tinned to prevent rusting. . . . With an 80 horse-power Gnome engine a speed of 70 miles per hour is attained. . . .'

We must not forget, however, that at any rate until 1920 it seemed at least as likely that the future would lie with airships. The first rigid airship was built in this country between 1909 and 1911, but it was a failure and its successor, the R 9, was not ready until 1916. Rigid, non-rigid and semi-rigid airships had been the subject of experiment ever since the eighteen-seventies; the French early had an airship like an Atlantic liner—550 feet in length—which maintained a regular passenger service for a time, but the German *Graf Zeppelin* was probably the most widely known and most successful. In all of these, one or several gondolas hung from the gas-filled envelope and they were propelled by engines in the gondolas. The R34 flew to America and back in 1919, taking 108 hours on the outward journey and 75 hours to return. But the R101 crashed in France with the Secretary of State for Air on board and she has had no successor. May we perhaps here quote Masterman's prophecy written in 1909: 'At best, any large accomplishment of flying must mean an increased hustling and speeding up of human life; more hurry, more bustle, more breathlessness, more triumphant supremacy of material things.'

About the turn of the century radio-activity and electrons were discovered and electron paths were photographed. The electrical theory of matter began to displace the chemists' previous granular theory. In 1921 Rutherford and Chadwick carried the transmutation of elements by electron bombardment a step farther and were successful in breaking up the complex atoms of a number of elements. In the 'twenties men began to exercise their minds on the potentialities of atomic fission: 'Sir Oliver Lodge

. . . points out that a body weighing one milligramme, travelling with the velocity of light, would possess energy amounting to 15,000,000 foot-tons and Sir William Crookes remarked that a gramme moving with the same speed would be capable of lifting the whole British Navy to the top of Ben Nevis.'[1] It is worth remembering that in (say) 1955 the possibility of travelling by rocket into space seemed equally remote to us. The story of the development of atomic research under the pressure of war and fear and of the successful controlled release of atomic energy need not be repeated here. But it is interesting that in the American underwater test at Bikini in 1946 the 26,000-ton battleship *Arkansas*, deliberately left in the trial area, was in fact lifted out of the water and for a brief space hung poised in the air before sinking. Heat from the experimental atomic pile at Harwell was first utilised in November 1951 and electricity generated in the world's first atomic power station was fed into the ordinary grid in 1958. But enough has been said to demonstrate the tempestuous rate at which all this has come about.

Henry Ford started the mass production of cars after 1909 and introduced the conveyor-belt system. Now it is widely adopted in industry and trade and also for the sedate movement of streams of human beings from one level to another. What is new, however, is its combination with various electronic devices. These make it possible for a stream of articles to be scrutinised and unsatisfactory specimens rejected, or sorted according to colour, shape or other characteristics, all without human intervention. Or varying components can be brought forward from storage areas to the assembly line by electronic devices, which will carry out an intricate series of previously memorised operations in the correct sequence and at the right time. This means, for instance, that at B.M.C. works near Birmingham there is a large tunnel in which components are moving forward in uncanny rhythm suspended from overhead rails with no human being in sight. When Ford erected their new Cleveland plant, electronic brains and self-operating machines, run by 250 workers, turned out in one day twice as much as was formerly produced by 2,500 workers.[2] These machines will carry out a whole series of

[1] Cressy, *op. cit.*   [2] *Economist*, February 1955.

different operations, proceeding from one to the other without human intervention and checking the correctness of their own work; such as the machine which cuts the cardboard, makes the boxes, fills them with sugar, checks, and seals them–stopping itself if it notices something wrong. Milk is now handled only by machines, from udder to bottle, and the bottle itself is one of an endless series turned out by a machine which needs only to be fed with liquid glass and compressed air. Typical of this modern world are the power stations with their rows of massive turbo-generators humming steadily with no human being in sight, or the relatively simple washing-machine which washes the clothes, dries them and then stops itself when its task is done– sometimes making a remark to draw attention to the fact.

As a result of modern science and industry the ordinary town-dweller now very seldom gets really wet or cold or hungry, or goes out in the dark, or walks more than a quarter of a mile at a time, except deliberately for exercise. In America it is not un-common for the wealthier city dweller even to spend the greater part of the twenty-four hours in 'conditioned' air–that is, air which has been sieved, dried and warmed–or cooled–before he breathes it. Manufacture and more recently agriculture are carried on by machines. The next step, and one we are in process of taking, will be for us to become inactive spectators in our factories.

Computers carry out intricate calculations at the speed of an electric current. They are used in industry for stock control (working out the rate of sale and necessary replenishment of many items in each of a chain of retail stores), for the payment of wages and for summarising great numbers of detailed calculations. In science they permit calculations which would previously never have been attempted because, by the unaided human brain, they would have taken so long and cost so much. The speed of computers (a British invention) makes it possible to calculate almost instantly the interaction of a number of variables and this leads to their military use in aiming projectiles at targets approaching at immense speeds. Computers are also used more happily to tabulate examination results.

10

The Social Revolution
Since 1900

I N tracing the development of the Welfare State since the beginning of the century we might start with Beatrice Webb. She was one of the nine daughters of Richard Potter–a wealthy businessman, for ten years president of the Grand Trunk Railway of Canada and a fairly typical upper-middle-class, Victorian paterfamilias. All of Beatrice Potter's eight sisters made the eminently 'satisfactory' marriages which their charm, intelligence and social position led their friends to expect. It seems that Beatrice might at one time have become Joseph Chamberlain's second wife, but she chose in 1892 to marry a lower-middle-class Socialist, Sidney Webb. Thus began that intimate and perfect working partnership by which Sidney and Beatrice Webb were able to produce great multi-volume histories of English local government and of trade unionism, to found the London School of Economics and Political Science in the University of London, to launch the weekly paper *The New Statesman*, to inspire the Fabian Society for a generation, and, as 'clerks' to the Labour Party, to contribute quite disproportionately to the ideas which underlay the domestic legislation of the Labour Government in 1945.[1] The partnership lasted until 1943, when it was dissolved by the death of Beatrice Webb. After her death the Order of Merit was conferred upon her husband. This distinction is still confined to men, but the aged Sidney Webb (then Lord Passfield) was assured that it was the work of the partnership which was thus recognized.

---

[1] Two hundred of the 394 Labour M.P.s who were successful in 1945 were members of the Fabian Society.

Just before its demise in 1905 the Conservative Government appointed a Royal Commission to consider the working of the Poor Law, and one of its members was Mrs. Sidney Webb. The formidable nature of the partnership, working through Mrs. Webb, quickly became apparent to the officials of the Poor Law Division of the Local Government Board. The relief of poverty was still in 1905 subject to the principle of 'less eligibility' which had been formulated in 1834, its application modified only to some extent in practice by the passage of the years and the development of the Victorian conscience. In principle, the determination of even the least fortunate workingman not to seek poor relief was to be fortified by the knowledge that so long as he could keep going somehow he was still better off than the most fortunate pauper. How dark was the shadow cast by the workhouse it is difficult for this generation to conceive, but it was intended to be dark. Mr. James Davy, head of the Poor Law Division, said in evidence before the Royal Commission that the pauper must suffer 'first the loss of personal reputation (what is understood by the stigma of pauperism); secondly, the loss of personal freedom which is secured by detention in a workhouse; and thirdly, the loss of political freedom by suffering disfranchisement'. (No person in receipt of poor relief could vote.) In the workhouse 'the work should be both monotonous and unskilled. . . . You have got to find work which anybody can do, and which nearly everybody dislikes doing. . . .' And again, 'the unemployed man must stand by his accidents; he must suffer for the general good of the body politic'. This was the official philosophy of the early years of the century, and its practical working has been described in the more seamy quotations of our first chapter. From these beginnings was to develop the Welfare State.

After four years' deliberation the Royal Commission recommended the break-up of the old Poor Law. But the rather colourless report of the majority has been overshadowed in history by the famous Minority Report, actually written by Sidney Webb and signed by Beatrice Webb, George Lansbury and two others. It is one of the great State papers of our time, for, scorning palliatives, it dissects the *causes* of poverty and is thus the parent of the legislation which has culminated in the Beveridge Report,

National Insurance and a National Health Service. The Minority Report recommended that old age should bring with it a State pension, and already in 1908 a pension of 5s. a week had been enacted for those past work and without means. It recommended that poverty caused by excessively low wages should be tackled by determining a national minimum wage, below which no employer might squeeze his hands, no matter how keen the competition for a job. As an experiment, the Trade Boards Act of 1909 laid down a minimum wage for a small number of exceptionally 'sweated' trades, and its principle has since been applied to others. The Minority Report recommended further that needy children, the sick and disabled should be assisted by the local authorities through their public health and educational services, while the unemployed were to be relieved by public works.

In three successive Acts of Parliament the Liberal Government which had come into office in 1906 limited the employment of children outside school hours, permitted–but did not oblige–the local authorities to provide free meals in school for children too undernourished to be teachable, and provided that children should be medically inspected in school. One has only to look at the school photographs of the time to see why these Children's Acts were called for; they reveal a world remote from the school world of to-day and a change of which we can only be proud, although its beginnings were sharply contested by many well-meaning people at the time. The first labour exchanges were set up in 1909 and incidentally mark William Beveridge's early preoccupation with unemployment. In 1911 the Liberal Government brusquely disappointed Webb hopes by passing the first National Insurance Act on a basis which demanded contributions from both employers and workers and to only a smaller extent from the State, leaving the benefits to be administered by private insurance companies and friendly societies (including those run by trade unions). The insurance also brought a claim on the services of certain listed doctors–'the panel doctors'–where hitherto the needy had been wholly dependent on the doctor paid by the Poor Law guardians. The same Act provided experimental unemployment insurance in a few trades.

With that the reforming impetus of the Liberal Government

was spent: as we have seen, the last turbulent years before 1914 were filled with other strange and more violent preoccupations. In 1920 insurance against unemployment was extended to the majority of wage-earners (and to salaried staff below a certain level), although domestic servants, agricultural workers, civil servants and railwaymen were excluded on account of their greater security of tenure. The pensions granted in 1908 were 'as of right', without payment of any contribution, but a beginning was made in 1926 with State retirement pensions to which the worker contributed by paying premiums during his active life. In 1929, twenty years after the Report of the Poor Law Commission, the guardians were eventually abolished, the ancient Poor Law disappeared and the relief of destitution became one of the duties of the local authorities.

Only five years later the rising level of social awareness and the massive unemployment of the 'thirties combined to engulf the last of the principles enunciated by Mr. Charles Davy in 1905. It was admitted that the man who obviously could not find work, and who had exhausted his claims under unemployment insurance, had nevertheless an ultimate claim on the State, and the Unemployed Assistance Board was made responsible for him. No longer must the unemployed man 'stand by his accidents' and seek ordinary poor relief as a pauper 'for the general good of the body politic'.

In 1942 Mr. Churchill's wartime Coalition Government published Sir William Beveridge's famous report on social insurance, in which he outlined plans for striking at want, disease, ignorance, squalor and idleness. One of the White Papers issued two years later to set out the Government's schemes for implementing the Beveridge proposals opens with the following passage in all the weight of official prose: 'The first duty of Government is to protect the country from external aggression. The next aim of national policy must be to secure the general prosperity and happiness of the citizens. To realise that aim two courses of action must be followed. The first is to foster the growth of the national power to produce and to earn. . . . The second is to plan for the prevention of individual poverty resulting from *those hazards of personal fortune over which individuals have little or no control.*'[1] This is the social revolution, and what is revolutionary is the removal, as by a solvent, of the stigma of pauperism, the recognition that poverty is by no means always the individual's own fault. The doctrine of a national minimum, of a net stretched out to catch each of us at a level below which we are not allowed to fall is a peculiarly 'Webb' contribution to our social thought.

The single insurance contribution, levied weekly and at a fairly high rate, now entitles each of us to a complete health service, without payment and according to need,[2] to relief in the event of unemployment, to a retirement pension and to a weekly contribution towards the upbringing of every child after the first. Furthermore it is the duty of the National Assistance Board to prevent want when insurance payments are insufficient or exhausted. But the atmosphere is pervasive and it is often forgotten that in addition to the national scheme very many private firms now have their own schemes, under which they contribute towards the cost of additional pensions for their employees or provide subsidised housing, meals, holiday homes or sports facilities. The 'density' of the present social services may be gauged from an amusing incident quoted by Mr. Donnison when a probation officer called at a house to find the mother already being interviewed by a school welfare officer, a mental health officer, a boarding-out officer from the Children's Department, and a city councillor. All five had arrived by coincidence at the same moment. The N.S.P.C.C., the Health Department, the Housing Department and the Family Service Unit were also all in touch with this family.[3]

What is the effect of all this? Mr. Rowntree made his first famous survey of poverty in York in 1899. He repeated the survey in 1936 and again in 1950. Approaching one-third of the cases of poverty were due in 1936 to unemployment and another one-third to inadequate wages. In 1950 the first cause had disappeared and the second accounted for only 1 per cent of the cases. Now two-thirds of the remaining poverty is due to old age. But there

---

[1] Cmd. 6550, 1944. My italics.
[2] Except for a contribution towards the cost of dentures and spectacles.
[3] D. V. Donnison, *The Neglected Child and the Social Services* (Manchester University Press, 1954).

is no room for complacency. A survey carried out in 1963 found that 'there are now more segments of the population below the British Medical Association standard (of adequate nutrition) than in 1950'.[1]

The nation's expenditure on the social services rose from £36 million in 1901 to £745 million in 1952;[2] and even if each earlier pound was worth £3 10s. at the later date, this is nevertheless a change of revolutionary size. In 1900 the number of civil servants in the two departments concerned, the Board of Education and the Local Government Board, was 1,870. In 1952 62,460 were employed in the Ministries of Health, Housing, Education, National Insurance and Pensions, and by the National Assistance Board. The whole apparatus of the State has swollen immensely with the revolutionary expansion of its functions. From defence, the preservation of law and order and some regulation of industry and working conditions, its functions have expanded to include the active promotion of welfare and the active promotion of trade.

It would be wrong to regard this as having been achieved (or perpetrated) by one political party, for it has been in the atmosphere of the times and has been the work of all three parties, starting with the Education Act of 1902, to go back no farther.[2] Between the wars it was, however, the Conservative Party which introduced protection, and the nationalisation of coal, electricity, gas and railways was the work of the Labour Government which came into power in 1945. This was the first Labour Government of the country's history not dependent on Liberal support but possessed of its own absolute and indeed overwhelming majority over the other two parties. (Or rather one should say over the Conservative and what remains of the Liberal Party, for the great Liberal majority of 1906 had forty years later been replaced by the great Labour majority of Mr. Attlee's Government.) Much of the essentially Fabian-Webb programme of the Labour Party had been carried out by the middle of the century.

[1] P. Townsend, *British Journal of Sociology*, vol. XIII, no. 3, 1962.
[2] These and the following figures in the text are from *The Economist*. (In the year 1963–4 expenditure in England and Wales on education, excluding school meals and milk, totalled nearly £1,200 million.) Local Government, housing and social services cost £3,236 million in 1966–7.

Nationalisation has not realised the early syndicalist dream of workers' control. Indeed the trade unions have spoken with a divided voice on this subject, only the miners and the railway-men consistently demanding that at least half the directorate of their industries should consist of workers' representatives. The Labour Party, under the influence of Mr. Herbert Morrison, inclined to the view that publicly owned industries should be managed by boards representing the public in general, and in effect the directorates set up by Mr. Attlee's Labour Government included eminent trade-union leaders only in their personal capacity, with no direct representation of the workers. Such men as Lord Citrine, chairman of the Central Electricity Authority, first resigned their union appointments, and necessarily, for they could not acknowledge responsibility both to the general public and to the workers.

Yet the whole status of the working classes in society and of the trade unions representing them has been immeasurably raised. It is difficult for this generation to realise how hard the unions—which are now so powerful that they sometimes even threaten the liberty of their individual members—had to struggle for recognition, or that the railway companies and the ship-owners, right up to 1914, stood out obdurately against negotiating with any unions representing their employees. In 1897, when the Webbs published their book *Industrial Democracy*, some critics 'ridiculed the idea of attaching even so much importance to the workmen's organisations as to write a book about them'. Trade-union membership, which totalled 2½ million in 1910, was 4 million by 1914, 8¼ million in 1920 and—after a setback in the intervening lean years—over 8¾ million in 1965. At the same time the 1,314 small unions of 1894 have been replaced by fewer and larger amalgamations. In 1914 two rooms housed the staff—one secretary and one assistant—of the Trades Union Congress; forty years later the foundations were excavated for the Trades Union Memorial Hall, one of London's major buildings and well able to compete in impressiveness with all but the largest palaces of capitalist industry. This external metamorphosis represents very fittingly the increase in the power and prestige of the trade-union movement. Now its representatives are frequently consulted by the Government on national economic issues and sit as equals with the employers' representatives.

Nevertheless the early struggle has left scars. The trade unions grew up in opposition to management and have always been linked with a political philosophy which proposes to abolish private industry. In this last they differ from their American counterparts, which certainly regard it as their task to get as much as possible out of the boss, but which have no quarrel in principle with the profit-making system which he operates. On the contrary, they welcome the bosses' larger profits with pride as both an achievement for which they are partly responsible and an opportunity for demanding pay increases, whereas here at home the profits of private industry are decried as a sign of its cloven hoof.

While there was considerable unemployment the bargaining power of a trade union was ultimately restricted by the fact that its members were replaceable. In the long term the employer had the whip hand. To-day this whip is no longer in the hand of the employer, but the national balance of payments with other countries has become one. A country which depends on its exports—and no longer has a great cushion of past savings to fall on—will cease to get a living if its prices get out of line with those of its foreign competitors. The responsible trade-union leaders cannot therefore push to its extreme the advantage which the present scarcity of labour gives them over the employers. The trade-union leaders have often exercised great restraint. Their new status brings a new responsibility, but while the national leaders are well aware of this, holding back often loses them control of their members in the factories—hence the 'unofficial strikes' led by shop stewards or unofficial committees.

The earliest unions consisted of skilled craftsmen and ignored the unskilled labourer at his side. Only later, with the increasing use of machinery, the skilled man began to take an interest in raising the status and pay of the unskilled who might be used to replace him. Now the point has been reached at which the wage difference between the general labourer and the man with skill and a burden of responsibility is probably less in several industries than it ought to be. Such is the strength of the present urge towards equality, which has also greatly improved the position of

L

the agricultural labourer. Agriculture is an industry which is now constantly in and out of the Government offices in Whitehall, for it is subsidised–in the year 1965–6 to the extent of about £295 million; the farmers have responded with an output more than 50 per cent above pre-war. Mr. Colin Clark calculated that between 1938 and 1949 the average farmer's 'real' income nearly doubled and the Government pledged itself in 1947 to maintain some kind of financial guarantee in order to protect British agriculture from wide price fluctuations and to ensure an adequate minimum income to the reasonably efficient farmer. All this, with greater security of tenure for the tenant farmer, is a minor social revolution, for it has made farming in Britain once again what it has not been in living memory, a profitable and attractive occupation.[1] No longer is the young man who wants to take up farming advised to emigrate to the Dominions although his well-being depends on Government support and he must wonder how he will fare if Great Britain enters the European Common Market. It does not follow that the land-owner has profited equally. Although by 1950 average farm rents per acre were 24 per cent up on 1938 they were still lower than they had been in 1872, when a land-owning aristocracy still flourished.

The number of voters increased from under 7 million in 1900 (when the figures included the whole of Ireland) to 35 million fifty years later. But at the same time the control of the party over the individual Member of Parliament has become much more rigid, the issues infinitely more complex, so that laws are now often passed merely as skeletons, leaving their effective detail to be filled in by the Civil Service. The result is that public control over government is less effective now than it was when the functions of government were but a fraction of their present size. If this expansion of government has robbed the achievement of universal suffrage of some of its fruits, it has also had a further and most striking effect in increasing the proportion of our income which is spent for us by the Government. In 1900 about 5 per cent of the national income was taken in taxation.

---

[1] Incidentally, it is now a highly mechanised occupation, with 300,000 tractors on the farms in 1950 as against 55,000 in 1939 and an increase in combine harvesters from 150 to 13,500 in the same period.

By 1910, after the Liberal social reforms, it was 8 per cent; by 1938 it was three times as much. In 1952, if we include local taxation and compulsory insurance contributions, the Government was clawing in and spending 42·5 per cent of national income (38·4 per cent without insurance contributions). The Budget, which in 1898 was passed at £102 million, had nearly doubled by 1913, had been multiplied nearly tenfold by 1938 and well over sixtyfold by 1964 (but it must be remembered that the value of each £1 is not what it was).

There are three main effects. When public expenditure was 5 per cent of national income it was no more than the necessary outlay on maintaining the public household. Now that the proportion is so much bigger it has become a method of setting the tone for the whole economy. More important: now that so much of our income is spent for us by the Government in health services, subsidies and pensions—and now that everyone over 21 has a vote—there is a certain temptation for each party to buy votes by promising ever more generous social services. Now also the social services have ceased to redistribute from rich to poor, for all but the lowest incomes must pay so much tax that it is calculated that they themselves pay for the benefits they receive. And the third effect springs in part from the second, because money can be increased at will but not so the solid material goods which the money should buy, and the result of too much money chasing too few goods is simply to inflate prices.

Inflation has eroded the value of money, so that the pound of 1962 bought only about as much as 6s. 6d. in 1938, while the 'cost of living' (which is variously defined) rose about 50 per cent even between 1946 and 1950. The value of money has never been constant—it has always suffered from war-time inflations and was affected by the great gold discoveries in the Klondike and the Rand—but previously change has been almost imperceptible, like the movement of a glacier. In this half-century the measuring-rod has visibly shrunk in our hands as we have attempted to use it, so that all of us, not only economists, are aware of its instability.

The vast increase in public expenditure has caused a correspondingly massive rise in the rates of taxation. The standard rate of tax on earned income was 9d. in the pound in 1906, 1s. 2d.

in 1913, 6s. in 1917, down to 5s. 6d. in 1938, up to 10s. (50 per cent) in 1942, and then down again to 9s. 6d. and 8s. 3d. Super-tax on the higher incomes was levied at 6d. in 1913, at 6s. in 1917, and rose ultimately to 9s. 6d. in every pound on the largest incomes. The higher incomes have paid tax at a higher rate ever since Lloyd George was Chancellor of the Exchequer. As taxation has tremendously increased with the growing needs of the State, so has the effectiveness of this device increased in like measure as a means of equalising incomes. It has been fortified too by what Gladstone caustically termed 'death duties', the tax levied on a man's estate before it passes to his heir. Between 1930 and 1938 the State took one-fifth of a fortune of £100,000 and one-half from the happy heir to £1 million. In 1948 the rate was raised to half of £100,000 and to four-fifths (in practice, owing to the method of assessment, sometimes the whole) of his inheritance from the unlucky heir to £1 million. Each of these tax increases has been hailed as the end of the world, as a crippling and impossible burden on industry and trade. Although the burden is great the world has gone on. Nevertheless these changes have marked the end of *a* world, of the world as our grandparents knew it.

To what extent has all this reduced privilege? The effect on the distribution of capital is striking, but not as rapid as one might have supposed. It has been calculated that in 1911–13 1 per cent of the population owned 65 per cent of all personal property, in 1926–8 57 per cent, ten years later 55 per cent, and in 1951–6 42 per cent.[1] The effect on yearly income is more rapid. In 1901 Professor Bowley estimated that 1·1 per cent of the population enjoyed 30 per cent of the income. By 1929–35, according to Mr. Colin Clark's calculations, the most wealthy 1·5 per cent claimed not more than 23 per cent of the income. In 1910 an individual with an income of £100,000 a year–and there were such people–had £94,000 left after tax. To-day he has about £6,000. In 1938 the highest income after tax was about twenty-eight times the lowest which paid tax; by 1948 it was about thirteen times the lowest, which itself had hardly changed. Finally,

[1] *Equality* (Allen & Unwin, 5th edn., 1964), which is also the source of most of the figures which follow.

and most striking, in 1938 7,000 people still enjoyed incomes of £6,000 or more after paying tax, whereas by 1950 there were only about 60 such people. The redistribution of income has been a good deal more striking than that of capital. 'Long years of economic depression, a civilians' war, rationing and "fair shares for all", so-called "penal" rates of taxation and estate duty, and "The Welfare State" have made little impression on the holdings of great fortunes. . . . Wealth still bestows power, more power than income, though it is probably exercised differently and with more respect for public opinion than in the nineteenth century.'[1] Moreover, recent studies reveal that in Britain, as in America, the movement towards more equal shares for all has been arrested since the middle of the century.

In this welter of statistics some further figures may be endured. The 1951 census of England and Wales revealed 178,000 resident domestic servants in private households: all that remained of the 706,800 of 1931. This is the attenuation of privilege—even the well-to-do can no longer count on personal service. But class differences remain: in 1947–8 an enquiry showed that 20 per cent of those earning £10 a week or more bath daily, as against only 1 per cent of those earning not more than £3.

The most important advantage conferred by privilege is the greater opportunity it gives its possessors to make the most of their natural abilities. For the poor there was in 1900 no secondary education; they left school at 12; the average number of pupils per teacher was 48 and each pupil cost the State 56s. a year. By 1913 about 174,000 children were getting secondary education with the aid, if not at the sole expense, of the State. In 1939 this figure had risen to 470,000, and since shortly after the end of the Second World War all our children have been entitled to secondary education free up to at least the age of 15, with an overall average in all types of school of 27 pupils per teacher in 1950 (although many classes are still far larger) and an average outlay of £51 per pupil.

There are several different kinds of secondary school. There is firstly the education which those who can afford it will

[1] From the Introduction by Professor R. M. Titmuss to the 1964 edition of *Equality*.

pay for if they cannot get it otherwise. Alongside this are the free secondary schools, whose ladder stretches right up to the entrance of the universities. In 1894 the odds against a child in an English elementary school gaining a scholarship to a grammar school were 270 to 1; by 1914 the odds against the child in a public elementary school in England or Wales getting free grammar-school type education to the age of about 18 were only 40 to 1, by 1920 21 to 1, by 1934 11 to 1, twenty years later about 4 to 1. After the war there was a rigid division between grammar schools, and secondary modern schools for those who had failed to clear the hurdle of a 'sorting out' examination at the age of eleven. The grammar schools kept their children up to 18 and gave them the academic basis for professional skills; the secondary modern schools, although an exciting first experiment in secondary education for all, sent out most of their children to wage earning at fifteen. This division, with its tendency to determine the fate of all but the most intelligent and pertinaceous at the age of eleven is now breaking down.

Nevertheless there is still a long way to go before the poorest of the publicly provided schools in the poorest areas are brought up to the level of the best in the best areas and all up to the standard—in terms of the number of pupils to each teacher, of equipment and amenity—of the *best* privately provided schools (not that all fee-paying schools are good). Proper training of technicians in industry also lags behind, although there is now a movement to improve it.

The child who has fortunately been at school till 18, who has the brains and the staying power and parental backing can now be almost certain of a university or technical college course, for which his fees will be paid, and he will be supported while studying. This is a movement which is twice blessed: once because it is removing injustice and again because the community so badly needs the ability which was previously wasted and untrained.

Where does this leave us? This is a society in which most people are aware of the need for greater equality and a fairer distribution of opportunities, but also gradually realising that wealth and the power it gives is less easily spread than at one time appeared, since wealth can be subdivided by trusts and gifts and other devices within family groups, without diminishing the privilege it conveys to those within the group. It is a society from which the extremes of ostentation and of abject poverty of the century's earlier years have disappeared. For the bulk of the people in the middle, and many more people are in the middle than in 1900, daily life, its stresses and its pleasures, are more equal, social differences far less obtrusive. The 'social revolution' has lost its impetus since mid-century, but a revolution since 1900 there has been.

This is a society now anxiously seeking increased efficiency in a competitive world, well aware of the need for technical skill and training, trying to solve its social problems by increasing its material wealth. We hope that 'such pockets of poverty and residual distress as still prevail will in time automatically . . . succumb to the determination of growth',[1] but are aware also that the latest automatic machines may now be replacing workers and concentrating capital in fewer hands. It is a society in which the younger people are rather conscious of their role, many of them anxious at last to escape from the old class divisions, to find each other as individuals. Perhaps they will also find a way of life which gives them sufficient material abundance without sacrificing the end of full living–and something of grace in living–to acquiring the means.

---

[1] Titmuss, Introduction to *Equality*, 1964. (He is not confident of this happening automatically).

A Skeleton of Dates

1899–1902 Boer War.

1900   Labour Representation Committee formed.

1901   Death of Queen Victoria. Accession of Edward VII.

1902   Education Act. Anglo-Japanese Treaty.

1903   Women's Social and Political Union founded.

1904–5   Russo-Japanese War.

1904   Anglo-French Entente.

1906   Liberal Government. Trade Disputes Act. Workmen's Compensation Act.

1909   Lloyd George's 'People's Budget'. Report on the Poor Law. Union of South Africa Act.

1910   Death of Edward VII. Accession of George V. Two general elections.

1911   Parliament Act. Industrial disputes. National Insurance Act. Agadir Crisis. Chinese Revolution.

1912–13   Balkan Wars.

1912   Home Rule Bill.

1914–18   First World War.

1914   Egypt declared a British protectorate.

1917   America enters the war. Russian Revolution.

1918   Representation of the People Act. Education Act.

1920   Unemployment Insurance Act. League of Nations established. Battle of Warsaw.

1922   Irish Free State established. French enter Ruhr. Fascist dictatorship in Italy. Egypt declared an independent state.

1924   First Labour Government.

1925   Return to gold standard. Safeguarding of Industries Act.

1926   General Strike.

1927   Chiang Kai-shek Government established in China.

1929   Local Government Act. Second Labour Government. Collapse on New York Stock Exchange.

1930   Round Table Conference on India.

1931   Statute of Westminster. Gold standard abandoned. Japanese invasion of Manchuria.

1932   Import Duties Act. Imperial Economic Conference, Ottawa. Disarmament Conference opens.

1933   Hitler seizes power.

1934   Unemployment Assistance Board. Conscription in Germany.

1935   Government of India Act. Italian invasion of Abyssinia.

1936-9 Spanish Civil War.

1936   Death of George V. Accession and abdication of Edward VIII. Accession of George VI. Anti-Comintern Pact. Rhineland remilitarised.

1937-45 Sino-Japanese War.

1938   Germany invades Austria.

1939   Germany invades Czechoslovakia.

1939-45 Second World War.

1941   Germany invades U.S.S.R. Japan attacks U.S.A. U.S.A. enters war.

1942   Beveridge Report.

1945   Atomic bomb.

1946   National Insurance Act. National Health Service Act. Coal Industry Nationalisation Act.

1947   Transport Act. Electricity Act. Partition of India and Pakistan. Onset of 'Cold War'.

1948   Union of Burma established. India, Pakistan and Ceylon self-governing members of Commonwealth. Israel established. Communist Government in Czechoslovakia.

1949   People's Republic of China proclaimed.

1950   War in Korea.

1954   French defeated by Communist Viet Minh at Dien Bien Phu (Vietnam).

1955   Bandung Conference.

1956   Hungarian rising suppressed by U.S.S.R.
        The Suez 'incident'.

1957   'Sputnik' launched into space.
        Ghana (first British African colony) and Malaya gain independence from Britain; Indonesia from the Netherlands.

1958   European Economic Community established.

1960   France grants independence to twelve African states.

1961   First man in space (Russian).

1962   Cuban crisis. Algeria gains independence from France; the Congo from Belgium; Jamaica and Trinidad from Britain. China attacks India.

INDEX

GEORGE ALLEN & UNWIN LTD
London: 40 Museum Street, W.C.1

Auckland: 24 Wyndham Street
Bombay: 15 Graham Road, Ballard Estate, Bombay 1
Calcutta: 17 Chittaranjan Avenue, Calcutta 13
Cape Town: 109 Long Street
Karachi: Metherson's Estate, Wood Street, Karachi 2
New Delhi: 13-14 Ajmere Gate Extension, New Delhi 1
Sydney, N.S.W.: Bradbury House, 55 York Street
São Paulo: Avenida 9 de Julho 1138-Ap. 51
Singapore, South East Asia and The Far East: 36 Prinsep Street
Toronto: 91 Wellington Street West

ENGLISH SOCIAL DIFFERENCES

T. H. Pear

Writers on social psychology and sociology have seldom discussed the nuances of experience and behaviour which characterize English social divisions. Their studies would be helped by a fuller 'natural history' upon which generalizations and theories could be more securely based.

To this natural history the author has attempted to contribute, recording and discussing numerous observations of the English social scene in the 20th century. Included are significant facts connected with manners, etiquette, speech, clothes and fashion, sports and games, and the many varieties of school and university education. The belief that some public schools train character rather than intellect is examined in detail. Different current concepts, of class, stratum, status, élite, gentleman, and aristocrat are compared. By contributing a wealth of facts, many of them not described elsewhere, his book provides an absorbing supplement to the text-books and suggests profitable subjects for research. In no sense does it profess to be a social history, but it does draw the attention of some English and foreign observers, whose views of 'the English Character' are described in detail, to outstanding features of our present behaviour.

Demy 8vo. 2nd impression. 18s. net

SOME YOUNG PEOPLE

Edited by Pearl Jephcott

The report of an inquiry into adolescents' reactions to their local youth groups. Besides answering the question 'Who joins what?' (and two-thirds of these thousand youngsters of 14 to 17 were not members of any youth organisation) the book describes some of the hopes, pleasures and difficulties of such people as Frances, the chocolate packer, who has ambition to marry before long; and John, the carpenter's apprentice, whose passions are autocycling, pigeons and pigs. It also throws light on problems such as those presented by gangs and suggests the importance of 'my friends,' the closely-knit set who mean so much to the adolescent.

Demy 8vo. 12s. 6d. net

A SHORT HISTORY OF THE BRITISH WORKING CLASS MOVEMENT

G. D. H. Cole

Omnibus Edition. Small Royal 8vo. 25s. net

HISTORY OF THE HOMELAND
Henry Hamilton

The aim of this book is to deal with the history of some of the things that matter most to people to-day. Its plan, therefore, is novel. It does not attempt to treat history chronologically. Instead it traces the background of social questions which are of burning topical interest to the ordinary citizen today. It deals with Human Needs. There are chapters on the Land, on Food, on Dress, on Health. It records the Rise of Capitalism in Britain and America. There are chapters on Money, Commerce, the Specialist in British Society, the Labour Movement, the Place of Women in Society, and Communications. It deals also with the British Empire—its Beginnings, the Growth of the Dominions, Economic Imperialism in Africa, Slavery and the Employment of Native Labour. It recalls the story of Government, Social Security, Education, and the struggle for Freedom of Thought and Freedom of Person.

Demy 8vo. 18s. net

THE BRITISH CONSTITUTION
H. R. G. Greaves

'From one point of view a contribution to academic literature and from another a distinguished addition to the literature of party politics. . . . Never fails to be stimulating.' *Spectator*

Cr. 8vo. Fourth impression. 15s. net

THE BRITISH APPROACH TO POLITICS
Michael Stewart

'This important volume is a book for which there should be a big demand . . . Many thousands of people who take an intelligent interest in contemporary politics would benefit by a study of this volume.' *Aberdeen Press and Journal*

Demy 8vo. 6th impression. 18s. net

Understanding the Modern World

YESTERDAY

Kathleen Harston

'Here is history with the immediacy of the weekly illustrated journal. Here verily is history as our grandfathers would tell it—if they had the pen of a fluent journalist, the memories of all the newspaper files, the sketching ability of a Bernard Partridge, and a completely ubiquitous camera. The story of the last eighty years is told through the experiences of an ordinary family . . . scores of excellent pictures . . . if you believe that history for the secondary modern pupil must "come alive", then you will have good reason to be grateful to Kathleen Harston and her publishers.' *Teachers' World*

COUNTRY LIFE THROUGH THE AGES

E. B. Watson and J. I. Carruthers

Making great use of illustrations and drawings the authors present a spirited and attractive outline of agriculture and country life from Celtic times until today. The Roman villa, the Dark Ages, Anglo-Saxon advances, the Three-Field system, the Norman Conquest, the Manor, the Monastery, Tudor, Stuart and later development are all portrayed by two very experienced teachers.

TOWN LIFE THROUGH THE AGES

R. W. Morris

'Its purpose is clear and the broad periods of architecture and civic development are described in abundant detail. Packed with facts, the book is well worth having in the library.' *The Times*

COMPLETE LIST OF THIS SERIES ON APPLICATION

$9\frac{1}{2}''$ x $7\frac{1}{2}''$. Library Edition. 5s. net each

---

GEORGE ALLEN AND UNWIN LTD